Joe McDonald
38 Marwill St
Albany N.Y.

Joe McDonald
38 Marwill St

From
Andrew & Elizabeth
Father's Day
6/18/95

The Best of
MGM

1

2

3

4

5

The Best of
MGM

ARS GRATIA ARTIS

In the splendor of wide screen, 70mm. and full stereophonic sound!

DAVID O. SELZNICK'S PRODUCTION OF MARGARET MITCHELL'S

"GONE WITH THE WIND"

CLARK GABLE
VIVIEN LEIGH
LESLIE HOWARD OLIVIA de HAVILLAND

A SELZNICK INTERNATIONAL PICTURE · DIRECTED BY VICTOR FLEMING · SCREEN PLAY BY SIDNEY HOWARD · METRO-GOLDWYN-MAYER INC · Music by MAX STEINER
RE-RELEASED BY METROCOLOR

Winner of Ten Academy Awards

ELIZABETH MILES MONTGOMERY

Brompton

First published in 1986 by
Brompton Books Corp.
15 Sherwood Place
Greenwich, CT 06830
USA

ISBN 1 85841 044 4

Printed in Hong Kong

For Daddy, who once played Andy Hardy
in *Skidding* on Redpath-Chautauqua.

CONTENTS

Previous spread:
1. The Wizard of Oz *(1939)*.
2. On The Town *(1949)*.
3. My Favorite Year *(1982)*.
4. High Society *(1956)*.
5. Mutiny on the Bounty *(1962)*.
6. Cat On A Hot Tin Roof *(1958)*.
7. Gone With The Wind *(1939)*.

Above: *Omar Sharif as Yuri Zhivago races along a train to find his family in* Dr Zhivago *(1965)*.
Page 6: *Clark Gable and Vivien Leigh in* Gone With The Wind *(1939)*.
Page 7: *Dorothy (Judy Garland) and her three companions run through the field of poppies in* The Wizard of Oz *(1939)*.

INTRODUCTION

METRO-GOLDWYN-MAYER still exists as a name, but is no longer a dream factory. Movies are still released under the M-G-M logo, but the style that once identified the M-G-M film in its heyday is missing. The roster of 'more stars than there are in heaven' no longer exists. The great collection of costumes and props that covered every style from Ancient Egypt to the Old West and beyond was auctioned off in 1970. The big sound stages are rented out for television and independent productions. The back lot which housed the standing sets for the Hardy's home town of Carvel, the main square of Verona and the deep tanks where Esther Williams swam has been sold to developers.

What lives, besides the memories of the actors and technicians that worked there, are the movies. In the years since its founding in 1924, M-G-M has made over 1700 films, which include some of the most popular of all time. Some of these are still bringing the M-G-M company revenue, as they are re-released to appear on television or on video. They include all the usual motion picture sub-species: westerns, adventures, some horror and science fiction, as well as romances, comedies and adaptations of the classics. Among them are such landmark films as *Gone With The Wind* (1939), *2001: A Space Odyssey* (1968) and both *Ben Hur*s (1925 and 1959). But M-G-M was also responsible for the first musical with sound, *Broadway Melody* (1929), the enchanting detective series based on Dashiell Hammett's *The Thin Man* (beginning in 1934) and the riveting drama, *Bad Day At Black Rock* (1957).

With such riches it is difficult to decide what constitutes 'the best.' There are some mediocre movies that are raised by a single brilliant performance, films that have come to symbolize an era and films that made a particular statement about a certain social problem. There are familiar films and some unfamiliar ones that it is hoped will pique the reader's interest and perhaps send him to the video shop, the television, or best of all, a revival on a big screen.

It would be futile to try to include all the movies in the Andy Hardy series, all the Tracy and Hepburn films, all of the Tarzans made by M-G-M (there were others), or all of the Nelson Eddy-Jeanette MacDonald operettas.

It was also necessary to eliminate most of the B pictures, those films made quickly on a limited budget to fill the bottom of a double bill. Another casualty has been most of the pictures made at the M-G-M studios in England.

When *That's Entertainment!* (1974) was released, *Variety* gave it a well deserved rave review, saying: 'While many may ponder the future of Metro-Goldwyn-Mayer nobody can deny it had one hell of a past.'

Here is a glimpse of that past.

Elizabeth Miles Montgomery

SILENTS
PLEASE

IN THE HISTORY OF Hollywood, the studios of Metro-Goldwyn-Mayer hold an extraordinary position. In the first place, their history is short. They were not there at the beginning, when the first moviemakers came west from New York, seeking the sun that made it possible to shoot movies year round.

The oldest of the three companies that made up M-G-M was Metro, or formally, the Metro Pictures Corporation, which was founded in 1915 from the ashes of a short-lived distribution exchange called Alco. As the motion picture craze spread throughout the United States and grew in popularity, the need for more new movies increased. Ex-members of the Alco Company invested a certain amount of money in the franchise with the idea that new films would be made by a series of companies that would distribute exclusively through Metro to the theaters in the exchange.

One of the members of the franchise was a distributor in Haverhill, Massachusetts, named Louis B Mayer, who was so entranced by the new medium that he decided to enter the production side for himself (and of course, distribute through Metro). The easiest way to do that successfully was to make movies with an already established star. The star Mayer chose to hitch his wagon to was Anita Stewart, who had made a sensation in the Vitagraph films, *A Million Bid* and *The Goddess*. Mayer promised her a company, Anita Stewart Productions, better directors and stories, a higher salary and a job for her new husband. After her first film for Mayer, *Virtuous Wives* (1919), was released and proved a popular hit, Mayer moved his organization and his new star to California.

At much the same time, the Metro Corporation ran into trouble. In an attempt to stay afloat, the company bought up all the franchises and started its own distribution. Once again close to bankruptcy, the stockholders looked to another company to bail them out, and in 1920 were bought by Loew's Incorporated, a growing chain of theaters throughout the United States and Canada. Again, the head of the new company felt that having a constant stock of new films to draw on exclusively could only be an advantage, especially since

Left: *Louis B Mayer (1885-1957), the independent producer who became the head of the M-G-M studios in California.*
Opposite right: Virtuous Wives *(1919) starred Anita Stewart.*
Opposite far right: *Rudolph Valentino in the famous tango scene from* The Four Horsemen of the Apocalypse *(1921).*
Previous spread: *Mélisande (Renée Adorée) bids farewell to Jimmy Apperson (John Gilbert) as Karl Dane looks on –* The Big Parade *(1925).*

protegé of the screenwriter June Mathis. The film had its premiere in New York in 1921, and became a sensation, as did the unknown who played Julio, Rudolph Valentino.

Other successes followed, including adaptations of the then popular novels *Scaramouche* and *The Prisoner of Zenda*. Metro also made a series of films with the most popular child star of the day, Jackie Coogan, and was responsible for the release of Buster Keaton's comedies.

The Goldwyn Pictures Corporation had been formed in 1916-17 by the well-known Broadway producers, Edgar and Archibald Selwyn and Samuel Goldfish, the ex-chairman of the board of Famous Players-Lasky, hence the combined name Goldwyn. Their first film was an adaptation of a romantic play by Edgar Selwyn's wife called *Polly of the Circus*. Several equally successful films followed including *Thaïs*, with Mary Garden, and *Carmen*, with Geraldine Farrar. In 1918, the Goldwyn company moved west to take over the vast Culver City studio of Thomas Ince's Triangle Films. The same year, Goldfish changed his name to that of

the studio of Famous Players-Lasky was about to charge a percentage of receipts rather than a flat rental fee for the use of their films.

What Loew's received for their money was the Metro studio in Hollywood, as well as the one in New York, and its roster of stars. Metro, in return, had the promise of a constant market for any and all the films Metro could produce. Marcus Loew wanted quantity, but he also expected a certain quality, and was willing to pay for it. Among the assets of the Metro company, in the preproduction stages, was an adaptation of the popular novel by Vincente Blasco-Ibañez, *The Four Horsemen of the Apocalypse*. The novel had been under consideration by most of the other Hollywood studios but its World War I setting made many feel it would be box-office poison. Loew's was willing to take the risk, even though the bulk of the film rested on the shoulders of an unknown

the company. By 1922, he had been forced out, and despite a prestigious line-up of stars and properties, the Goldwyn company was in trouble.

One of the board members of Goldwyn Pictures was the theatrical impresario, Lee Schubert, who was also a member of the board of Loew's Incorporated, the parent company of Metro. It was Schubert who had the novel idea of combining the two studios under one name and staff, thus insuring the production of the promised and necessary number of films. To run this new enterprise, the Loew's office chose Louis B Mayer, whose little studio on Mission Road had been a profitable venture, and whose managerial talents were undisputable. With Mayer came Irving Thalberg, the frail 'boy wonder,' who at the age of 24 already had an enviable reputation for intelligent movie production.

Another asset to the new studio was the independent company of Cosmopolitan Productions, which had been created by William Randolph Hearst to make movies starring Marion Davies. It was an advantage chiefly because of Hearst's enormous newspaper empire, though Miss Davies was a comedienne of great talent and charm.

On 24 April 1924, there was a formal dedication of the new company, and work began on a new roster of films to be presented under the old Goldwyn trademark of the roaring lion bearing the legend 'Louis B Mayer presents . . . a Metro-Goldwyn picture.' This soon became the better known 'Metro-Goldwyn-Mayer presents . . .', but the company was known as M-G-M.

One of the first independent productions to go before the

cameras was *He Who Gets Slapped* (1927), an adaptation of a play by the Russian dramatist Leonid Andreyev, which had been produced in New York by the Theatre Guild. Basically it was the psychological study of a renowned scientist who becomes a circus clown when his wife betrays him, but screenwriter Carey Wilson excised the slightly hazy philosophy and emphasized the circus background and the secondary romance between two bareback riders.

The director, personally selected by Louis B Mayer, was Victor Seastrom, a Swede who had come to the United States for the Goldwyn Company in 1921. The equestrienne heroine who is also loved by the clown was played by Norma Shearer, a Mayer contract player destined for better things. Recommended to Mayer by a friend on the East Coast, Shearer's previous experience included a stint as 'Miss Lotta Miles,' the trademark beauty of the Springfield Tire Company. Her first part for Mayer had been the ingenue lead in the film *Pleasure Mad*.

Her leading man was one of the silent screen's great lovers, John Gilbert, who had made his first film appearance as an extra in the Ince-Triangle film, *Matrimony* in 1915. His first film for M-G-M was an adaptation of an Elinor Glyn Ruritanian romance, *His Hour*, with Aileen Pringle. The pivotal part of the scientist-turned-clown was played by Lon Chaney, best known for his portrayal of the bell-ringer Quasimodo in *The Hunchback of Notre Dame* (1923) for Universal.

The plot was not free from certain melodramatic devices or the long arm of coincidence, especially in the denouement,

when the aristocrat (Tully Marshall), who had cuckolded Chaney, arrives at the circus and begins to take an interest in Shearer, almost to the point of a fate worse than death. Chaney allows a hungry lion to escape and it attacks and kills Marshall. Chaney also dies and the two lovers, Gilbert and Shearer, are free to marry.

Despite the less believable aspects of the story, it was well-received by the public, the fans responding to the romance between Gilbert and Shearer and the tragedy of Chaney. *The New York Times* called it 'a picture which defies one to write about it without indulging in superlatives . . . so beautifully told, so flawlessly directed that we imagine it will be held up as a model by all producers.' In any case, the new studio had its first hit.

Among the assets brought to M-G-M by Metro were the distribution rights to the films of Buster Keaton. Keaton, one of the three great clowns (with Charlie Chaplin and Harold Lloyd) of the silent screen, had been producing his brilliant one-, two- and seven-reelers at his own studio since 1920. Among these were such classics as his first, *One Week* (1920), *The Boat* (1921) and *Seven Chances* (1925).

The first film released by the new studio was *Sherlock Jr* (1924), an incredible stunt-filled fantasy about a daydreaming movie projectionist who yearns to be a detective. It is best remembered for the wonderful scenes when Keaton finds himself within the movie he is projecting. Keaton moves around the on-screen house until he is thrown out of the screen. Purposefully he climbs back in and finds himself outside. Preparing to sit on a garden bench to rest, he falls to the ground on a city street when the bench disappears. Sauntering along the street, Keaton suddenly comes to a cliff edge as the scene cuts once more. It was a brilliant and intricate piece of movie-making and fascinated contemporary film technicians more than the general public. It is still a *tour de force* but plays no part in advancing the rather gentle plot of the rest of the film.

The same year M-G-M also released *The Navigator*, with Keaton as a rather absent-minded millionaire cast adrift by spies on an ocean liner. It was his most successful production. Keaton originally hired Donald Crisp, later and better-known as a character actor, to direct, but as usual, Keaton himself was responsible for most of the direction. *The Navigator* costarred Kathryn McGuire as the girl who is kidnapped by cannibals when the liner reaches a desert (but not deserted) island. She is rescued by Keaton in a brilliant underwater sequence, one of the first in movie history. This scene was filmed three times, once in a tank which cracked under the weight of water and equipment, again off Catalina Island where the water proved too murky to shoot and at last in the cold but clear waters of Lake Tahoe, a tribute to Keaton's professionalism and doggedness in bringing his own comedic visions to the screen.

In 1922, shooting began on Polk Street in San Francisco on a Goldwyn Company film which would run in rough cut for 42 reels, or almost nine hours. The director managed to reduce it by half. Eventually veteran editor and screenwriter June Mathis managed to cut it further to just over two hours.

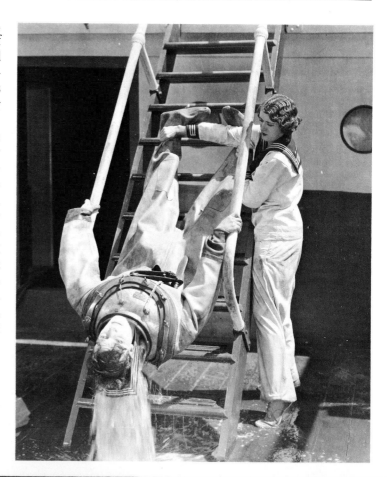

Right: *Gibson Gowland as the dentist McTeague in* Greed *(1925). Zasu Pitts (right) played his wife Trina.*
Right below: *John Gilbert embraces an unidentified player as Mae Murray studies his technique in* The Merry Widow *(1925).*

Opposite top: *Kathryn McGuire gives Buster Keaton a hand in* The Navigator *(1924).*
Opposite below: *Buster Keaton played a romantic projectionist in* Sherlock Jr *(1924).*

By this time, the Goldwyn Company was part of M-G-M, and so to the new studio fell the distinction of releasing Erich von Stroheim's masterpiece *Greed* (1924).

Based on *McTeague*, a novel by Frank Norris, *Greed* starred Gibson Gowland in the lead role, Zasu Pitts as his wife, Trina, and Jean Hersholt as Trina's cousin and former suitor, Marcus.

The plot of the movie follows Norris' novel exactly, but emphasizes the more brutal aspects of late nineteenth century lower middle class life. The quack dentist McTeague falls in love with one of his patients, an immigrant German girl named Trina. At the time of their engagement, Trina wins $5000 in a lottery. Following their wedding, which is depicted in a long, exaggerated and somewhat brutal scene, Trina becomes a miser, hoarding her prize, an action which feeds McTeague's resentment. At the same time, Trina's cousin Marcus, jealous of the marriage and what he views as Trina's fortune, exposes McTeague to the dental board and the dentist is forced to give up his practice.

Deprived of his livelihood, McTeague becomes a vagrant. Estranged from Trina, he eventually murders her in a drunken rage. He flees to Death Valley where he is tracked down by Marcus who wants to claim the reward money. Under the harsh sun of the desert they kill each other.

In a departure from his usual style, von Stroheim filmed each scene described by Norris, including every metaphor. Among the most memorable of these are the various shots of the caged lovebirds which McTeague had given Trina on their wedding day. To emphasize the sense of avarice which almost overwhelms the movie, von Stroheim had a number of frames hand-tinted with gold paint, although the film was, of course, made in black and white. Another departure was von Stroheim's decision to film inside an actual house in San Francisco, a technique which adds to the pervading sense of claustrophobia. The final scenes were actually shot on loca-

tion in Death Valley, which increased the stark reality of the last reels.

Even with the mass of cuts, M-G-M was unsure of *Greed's* reception, an opinion which was borne out by the reaction when the film was finally released in December 1924. Unaccustomed to such brutal realism, the critics, except for an enlightened few, hated it, and the public stayed away in droves.

Von Stroheim was disappointed with the new studio's inability to share his vision, being, in turn, unable to understand the studio's necessity to produce films that would be successful at the box office. His next and last film for M-G-M was an adaptation of *The Merry Widow* (1925) starring John Gilbert and Mae Murray, which emphasized the decadence

Left: *Francis X Bushman played the Roman tribune Messala in the first M-G-M version of* Ben Hur *(1925).*

Opposite: *The role of the innocent doughboy Jimmy Apperson in* The Big Parade *(1925), was an unusually unglamorous one for John Gilbert.*

of the Austro-Hungarian Empire, rather than the froth and romance. Again the film was overlong and again Irving Thalberg demanded major cutting before release. In a fury, von Stroheim left M-G-M for Paramount. His last directorial assignment was *Queen Kelly* (1928) with Gloria Swanson, which was not released until many years later. *Greed* remains, even in its truncated form, the best testament to von Stroheim's vision and talent.

Another major Goldwyn film had been in production at the time of the merger and this one was in even more difficulty than *Greed*.

General Lew Wallace's novel *Ben Hur: A Tale of the Christ* had been popular since it was published in 1880. An adaptation for the stage, featuring the chariot race on a treadmill, was first produced in 1899. The first film version, made without clearing permission, was a 1907 quick two-reeler which had taken advantage of a chariot race staged at Coney Island.

Hoping to restore its prestige and bank balance, the Goldwyn Company eventually obtained the film rights in 1922 from the theatrical producer Abraham Erlanger who had been presenting the play of *Ben Hur* since 1899, in return for 50 percent of the profits. June Mathis, then the head scenarist at Goldwyn, set to work on the screenplay, while casting began with the lead roles going to George Walsh as Ben Hur and Francis X Bushman as Messala. Charles Brabin, whose independent production *Driven* (1923) was considered a masterpiece, was signed to direct, and for 'authenticity' it was decided to make the picture in Rome.

Delays struck the production before it was truly begun. The cast and crew arrived in Italy to find unfinished sets and labor disputes. Eventually with 12 galleys instead of the promised 70, Brabin began to shoot the sea battle where the galley-slave Ben Hur rescues the Roman General Quintus Arrius, at Anzio.

Back in Hollywood, the merger that created M-G-M took place and responsibility for the expense of *Ben Hur* shifted to the new studio. After screening Brabin's rushes, Mayer and Thalberg resorted to drastic measures. They replaced George Walsh (who hadn't even appeared yet) with a rising Metro star Ramon Novarro. Brabin lost the directorship to Fred Niblo, and June Mathis, who had worked on the project since 1922, saw her screenplay thrown out, while Carey Wilson and Bess Meredyth set to work on another.

Even these changes didn't solve the problems of *Ben Hur*. Though satisfied with the interiors and much of the opening scenes at the Joppa Gate of Jerusalem, Niblo, the new director, was forced to reshoot the naval battle and the rescue of Quintus Arrius.

The climax of the film, the chariot race, was the responsibility of second unit director Reeves Eason, who was not able to begin shooting until the vast set for the arena at Antioch was completed. Even then, the Italian crew and extras managed to delay the shooting schedule.

With the movie already running way over budget, Mayer and Thalberg called the entire company back to California to complete filming, despite the necessity of rebuilding the vast sets they would leave behind in Italy.

While Niblo concentrated on his characters and the plot, using a number of wonderful miniatures to give grandeur to the outside shots, Eason was back at work on the race. The culmination of this labor occurred one Saturday and everyone in the film colony participated. To get the right sense of intensity, several races were run, with prizes being offered to the winners, since Eason planned to shoot his close-ups of Bushman and Novarro at another time. The crowd of extras, which included some of Hollywood's brightest future stars, threw themselves into their parts cheering and waving, while the action was being filmed by 42 cameras situated all over the set, behind columns and soldiers' shields and in pits dug into the racetrack itself. Approximately 53,000 feet of film was shot on that one day, out of a total of 200,000 expended on the chariot race. It would eventually be cut down to a sequence barely 750 feet long, which is still one of the most exciting pieces of film ever made, and brought the audience to their feet at the premiere in 1925.

The reaction to the rest of the film was also high, many critics citing in particular the tasteful depiction of Christ as only a hand sawing wood, or offering Ben Hur water or merely a footprint. They also praised the performances of Novarro, and Betty Bronson who appeared as the Madonna in the prologue.

Thalberg was so pleased that it was one of the three films in his lifetime which carried his name as a credit. Unfortunately the vast gross profit was wiped out by the cost and the enormous royalty Goldwyn had offered Erlanger. However, M-G-M would release the film several times over the years, including a very profitable reissue in 1931 with sound effects. From a Goldwyn disaster, M-G-M had scored a triumph.

One of the surprise hits of Broadway's 1924 season was *What Price Glory?*, a comedy set in France during World War I, by Maxwell Anderson and Laurence Stallings. When Irving Thalberg tried to buy the rights he found that the Fox Corporation had gotten there first. Nothing daunted, he engaged Stallings, a former Marine who had lost a leg at Belleau Wood, to write an original screenplay, feeling that 'the European war was big enough to support more than one movie.'

Thalberg envisioned a wartime love story, but director King Vidor wanted an action picture featuring an American Everyman. Stallings and screenwriter Harry Behn worked out a screenplay that was both. They called it *The Big Parade* (1925). The plot was a tried and true one. A rich man's son enlists in the AEF and is sent to France where he falls in love with a French peasant girl, marches into battle where his friends are killed and he loses a leg to shrapnel. When the war is over, he returns to France to find the girl.

As the doughboy, Jimmy Apperson, John Gilbert happily discarded his usual glamorous roles and under Vidor's direction gave an impressive and touching performance. His costar was Renée Adorée as the French milkmaid, Mélisande, and the cast was rounded out by Tom O'Brien and Karl Dane as the doughboy's friends.

Despite the gentle humor that pervades the scenes behind the lines, especially the one in which Gilbert introduces Adorée to chewing gum which she swallows, *The Big Parade* is best remembered for its battle scenes. Perhaps the most vivid of these is that of the American troops marching down a long straight road and through a sun-lit wood to almost certain death.

The Big Parade opened at the Astor Theater in New York and ran there for a record 86 weeks. The public loved it, but the critics were not unanimous in their praise, although Robert Sherwood wrote, '*The Big Parade* is a marvelous picture that can be ranked among the few great achievements of the screen. He [Vidor] has made war scenes that actually resemble war.' *The New York Times* agreed: 'A superior war picture . . . an eloquent pictorial epic of the world war. . . . It is a subject so compelling and realistic that one feels impelled to approach a review of it with all the respect it deserves. . . . The scenes are as perfect as human imagination and intelligence could produce.'

Though today it may be considered somewhat sentimental, *The Big Parade* laid a few of the ground rules and developed techniques that would be used again and again in war movies up to the present day.

Following the success of *He Who Gets Slapped*, Lon Chaney made a series of films for M-G-M including *The Tower of Lies* (1925), *The Monster* (1925) and *The Blackbird* (1926), in which Chaney played that stock character of horror films, the mad doctor. In 1925 he also starred in *The Unholy Three*.

Directed by Tod Browning, who would later direct *Dracula* (1930) for Universal, *The Unholy Three*, written by Clarence Robbins and Waldemar Young, was set in a circus where Chaney as Echo, a ventriloquist, and two of his fellow sideshow performers, the strongman Victor McLaglen and the midget Harry Earles, have become pickpockets, taking advantage and revenge on the people who have come to gawk at them. Also starring was Mae Busch as a more professional thief who encourages them to turn to more serious burglary and eventually murder.

The part of the ventriloquist called for Chaney to assume a series of disguises, and is best remembered for his remarkable appearance as an old woman, complete with gray wig, bonnet and full skirts. It is in this disguise that he gives himself away on the witness stand and is captured.

In 1929, the film was remade with sound as Chaney's first talkie. Jack Conway was the director, and the cast included Lila Lee, Elliot Nugent and once again Harry Earles as the dwarf. The disguises were augmented by Chaney's brilliant vocal impersonations. The film was an even greater success than its illustrious silent predecessor. Chaney had made the switch to talkies without any problem. Sadly, his first talkie was also his last, for he died of throat cancer two months after the picture was released.

M-G-M continued to attract major stars to its stock company, and one of those that joined in 1925 was Lillian Gish. Even then one of Hollywood's legendary stars, she was best known for the films she made with D W Griffith, *The Birth of a Nation* (1915), *Broken Blossoms* (1919) and *Way Down East* (1920). Among those she had made since were two co-starring a rising young English actor named Ronald Colman. The first of these, *The White Sister* (1923) was released by

Metro, and the second, *Romola* (1924), which also starred William Powell and Lillian's sister Dorothy, had actually been released by M-G-M.

Gish's contract allowed her to pick her own vehicles, and as her first M-G-M film, she chose *La Bohème* (1925), but with a script based more on the original stories in Henri Murger's *La Vie de Bohème* than the better known Puccini opera. Thalberg had given his new star the right to name her own director and was delighted when Gish picked King Vidor because she had been impressed by *The Big Parade*. She also

Above: *John Gilbert as the poet Rudolph comforts the dying Mimi (Lillian Gish) in* La Bohème *(1925).*
Opposite: Flesh and the Devil *(1926) was the first film to costar Greta Garbo and John Gilbert.*

Left: *In* The Unholy Three *(1925) Lon Chaney (center) disguised himself as an old woman.*

chose the costars in that film, John Gilbert and Renée Adorée to play the poet Rudolph, and the singer Musetta. She herself would play Mimi.

Like her mentor Griffith, Gish was a stickler for accuracy, and disapproved of the original set, which she described as a big beautiful house. Eventually, the little flower seller was seen living in a garret, but thanks to Hollywood production values, it was a large one. Gish also disapproved of the costumes, which were designed by Erté and made of new, stiff fabric. She had her own re-made in old silk, which she felt moved and hung correctly.

Gish had original ideas about the love scenes between Mimi and Rudolph, feeling that suppressed emotion would be more effective than fervent embraces. At this, Thalberg drew the line. The co-star was John Gilbert, and Gilbert's fans demanded love scenes. Gish gave in gracefully, but was heard to say, during the filming, 'Oh, dear, I've got to go through another day of kissing John Gilbert.'

She did get her own way about the death scenes. For accuracy, Gish spent time in a Hollywood hospital studying tuberculosis patients. During the filming she touched no liquids so that her lips would be properly parched. Her

diligence paid off, for the film was a great success in the United States, and even more popular in Germany where it ran for many years, under the title *Mimi*.

While Lillian Gish was working so carefully on *La Bohème*, she was being observed by a young actress who was making her first M-G-M film nearby. The film was *The Torrent* (1925) a lightweight melodrama about a Spanish peasant turned opera-singer, but the young actress was Greta Garbo.

Garbo had been discovered by Louis B Mayer when he saw the Swedish film, *The Story of Gösta Berling*, while traveling in Europe during the *Ben Hur* fiasco. He instantly signed Garbo and the director Mauritz Stiller to M-G-M contracts.

The Torrent was followed by a similar film, *The Temptress* (1926), and then another, *Flesh and the Devil* (1927). Once again the plot concerned a seductive and amoral woman who destroys the men who love her, before she herself dies. Such retribution was insisted upon by the censors and the front office. Stiller warned Garbo that she might become typecast in such parts if she kept accepting them. Partly for Stiller's sake, Garbo did not want to play the role, but she had been cast opposite John Gilbert, of whom she was an ardent fan.

In turn, Irving Thalberg had to persuade Gilbert to accept

his role in the movie. Gilbert was tired of his reputation as a great screen lover, which had been enhanced by his performances in *The Merry Widow* (1924) and *La Bohème* (1925). He felt, somewhat correctly, that nothing could compare with his part in *The Big Parade* (1924).

Almost from the moment the two stars met, they fell madly in love. And this passion was transmitted to the screen. Perhaps the translation was aided by the brilliant camera-work of William Daniels, who would remain Garbo's favorite cameraman throughout her career. Another asset was the direction of Clarence Brown, who, though he may have felt like a voyeur, incorporated horizontal love scenes, a Hollywood first, which increased the erotic impact of the film.

The public and the reviewers were stunned. The New York *Herald Tribune* critic wrote: 'Never before has John Gilbert been so intense in his portrayal of a man in love. Never before has a woman so alluring, with a seductive grace that is far more potent than mere beauty, appeared on the screen. Frankly, we have never seen in our career a seduction scene so perfectly done.' M-G-M may not have expected such a tremendous and profitable reaction to their new star, but Thalberg and Mayer were certainly willing to back her to the hilt. Unfortunately, Mayer's deep animosity to John Gilbert kept that actor from better parts until the untimely end of his career.

Another major feature of 1926 was an adaptation of Nathaniel Hawthorne's novel *The Scarlet Letter*, starring Lillian Gish as Hester Prynne. Adaptations of classic novels fit right in with Mayer and Thalberg's concept of raising the standard of the motion picture, and the denouement of *The*

Scarlet Letter, emphasizing guilt and retribution, was a favorite of Mayer. However, the aspect of adultery had placed it on a black list by women's clubs and the Catholic Church. Once again, Lillian Gish was willing to stand up for her movie. She wrote to the heads of many women's organizations and several dioceses, who agreed to lift the ban if she would be personally responsible for the film.

Lars Hanson, who had already played a doomed minister in *The Story of Gösta Berling*, was chosen to play Hester's lover Reverend Dimmesdale, and her husband, Roger Chillingworth, was played by an old friend from the Griffith company, Henry B Walthall. The director was Victor Seastrom, who managed to instill the film with an atmosphere of suspicion and superstition that was quite frightening, if not precisely Hawthorne. 'It's a real "A" picture,' said the salesmen, but as usual Gish was vindicated.

The Big Parade had not exhausted King Vidor's interest in Everyman. Having seen him through the war, Vidor wondered how the average man would survive in peacetime. With Thalberg's approval, Vidor and Harry Behn, who had worked on the script for *The Big Parade*, developed the story of a small town boy who goes to the city and barely manages to make a living. They called it *The Crowd* (1927). For his hero, Vidor knew he could not use a well-known star, and eventually settled on James Murray, a part-time M-G-M extra, who had the right lack of distinction and a nice, but average, face. To play the wife, Vidor chose an excellent actress, Eleanor Boardman, who happened to be his own wife.

To give the film the realism that Vidor felt was necessary, he used the technique devised by von Stroheim for *Greed*, and shot the exteriors on the streets of New York and outlying areas. At one point, the camera follows the young man from his arrival in Manhattan by ferryboat to an office

building, where the camera remains outside, moving up the exterior of the building until the hero is seen, as one of many clerks, through the window.

In a series of shots that have now become clichés, Vidor traces the life of an average couple through their petty triumphs and sorrows, sometimes slipping over into melodrama. The ending showed the young man, his wife and their child at a movie, enjoying the advertisement which had won the young man a bonus, before the camera moved back and they are lost in the rest of the audience. Mayer found it too down-beat, and insisted Vidor film an alternative that was more positive. Exhibitors were then given their choice of endings. As usual, the larger cities asked for the original, the rest of the country wanted a happy ending.

Vidor would finish his trilogy in 1934, with the release of *Our Daily Bread*, the story of farmers creating a cooperative farm. It was not a success and Vidor returned to purely commercial film making.

For several years, M-G-M had been making a series of light films, purporting to show the youth of the twenties at play. The most successful of these was *Our Dancing Daughters* (1928) and its major strength was the performance of its star, Joan Crawford. The plot of *Our Dancing Daughters* concerned Diana, the young flapper, whose wild life contrasts unfavorably with that of her friend Anne. In reality, it is Diana who is virtuous and idealistic and Anne (Anita Page) who is selfish and immature. Rich young Ben Black (Johnny Mack Brown) does not realize this until too late, i.e. after he has married Anne. Anne soon turns to drink and falls downstairs, killing herself, so that Diana and Ben can be reunited.

It was Crawford who turned this silly story by Josephine Lovett into a hit. And the film is still best known for the Charleston danced by Crawford, dressed only in her teddy. Her whole exaggerated personality seemed to fit the era and the film to perfection.

The film was such a success that it launched a series of similar pictures, *Our Modern Maidens* (1929) and *Our Blushing Brides* (1930), also starring Crawford, who by this time was probably sorry she had ever learned to Charleston.

Victor Seastrom and Lillian Gish worked together on one last film for M-G-M before Miss Gish's contract expired. This was *The Wind* (1928), a Western with a difference. Gish played a young girl traveling out west to marry, as she explains to a fellow passenger, Wirt Roddy (Montagu Love), who has taken an interest in her. On her arrival at the ironically named town of Sweetwater, she still faces a long buggy ride to her new home, which gives Seastrom an opportunity to show the constantly blowing wind, which intensifies the sense of isolation. When Roddy returns to the rough cabin and rapes her, she kills him and tries to dispose of the body outside, but the sand is continually blown away from the grave, revealing the body. The heroine is eventually driven mad.

It is a very stark movie made under very harsh conditions in the Mojave Desert, where the temperature would reach 120°F and melt the emulsion off the film. Eight aeroplane propellers were used to move the sand, and the hazards were increased by the sudden appearance of a real sandstorm.

Though today *The Wind* is considered one of Gish's masterpieces, it was not popular when first released. Again the ending was changed, to reconcile the heroine with her husband, (and, one presumes, her mind). Gish's films for M-G-M had not been the money-spinners the studio had hoped they would be, and the star and Thalberg decided to cancel her contract with one picture still to go. This had been planned as an adaptation of *Anna Karenina* to be called *Heat*. The film was finally made with Greta Garbo and John Gilbert, but the title was changed to *Love* (1928) when someone realized that the marquees across the United States would advertise 'Greta Garbo and John Gilbert in *Heat*.'

Filming had actually started with Ricardo Cortez, but the public reaction to *Flesh and the Devil* was so high, M-G-M decided to scrap everything that had been shot to date, and begin again with Gilbert as Vronsky. This modern-dress version of *Anna Karenina* is also renowned for having two endings, the original where she throws herself under a train, and a second, happy one, where several years later, following the death of Karenin, she and Vronsky are reunited. Exhibitors could have their choice.

Our Dancing Daughters, The Wind and *Love* were all made after the introduction of sound by Warner Bros. *Our Dancing Daughters* even had a music track added to it, for M-G-M was aware that a major change was coming to the movies, and they certainly intended to be part of it. The days of silence were numbered.

Below: *Greta Garbo and John Gilbert as the unhappy lovers in* Love *(1928), a modern-dress adaptation of* Anna Karenina.

Opposite: *Lillian Gish prepares to defend herself against her attacker (Montagu Love) in* The Wind *(1928).*

ALL TALKING,
ALL SINGING,
ALL DANCING

M-G-M WAS ONE OF THE last studios to move to sound, and they tested the waters of the new medium with care. The shift to sound film could not be accomplished overnight, and indeed, M-G-M, like other studios, continued to turn out silents for the theaters which had not yet undertaken the expensive conversion to sound equipment. However, little by little, the studio experimented, in the first instance by adding sound effects and synchronized music to completed silent films, such as *White Shadows in the South Seas* (1928), which was also the first M-G-M movie to include the roar of Leo, their trademark lion. Another half-measure on the road to sound was accomplished by reshooting scenes and adding dialogue to recently finished pictures. This was done with two recently finished pictures, *The Bellamy Trial* and *Alias Jimmy Valentine*.

However, when M-G-M made its first all sound picture, it did something brand new: *Broadway Melody* (1929), the first movie musical with sound. The idea had come from Major Edward Bowes, later an important radio personality, but then the executive manager of the Capitol Theater in New York, the largest of the Loew's first run houses. Bowes wanted a light romantic film to open the fall 1928 season and knew his audience wanted an 'all-talk' picture. Bowes also knew that many of the young people wanting to break into show business had a fairy-tale idea of theater life. So was born the 'backstage musical.' It was Irving Thalberg's idea to add the songs and dances, especially since he had two new song-writers under contract, lyricist Arthur Freed and composer Nacio Herb Brown.

Broadway Melody was the story of a vaudeville team of two sisters, Hank and Queenie Mahoney (Bessie Love and Anita Page), which breaks up when they both fall in love with the same rather caddish songwriter, played by Charles King. The simple plot was interspersed with musical numbers like 'You Were Meant For Me,' the title song and 'The Wedding of The

Above: Broadway Melody (1929) starred Anita Page, Bessie Love and Charles King.
Opposite top: The Hollywood Revue of 1929 (1929) used a jewel-box background for many of its chorus numbers.
Previous spread: Jean Harlow starred with Clark Gable in Red Dust (1932).
Opposite below: Nina Mae McKinney, here with Fannie Belle de Knight, starred in Hallelujah (1929).

Left: Monte Blue played a drunken doctor in the semi-sound, semi-documentary White Shadows in the South Seas (1928).

Painted Doll,' the last shot in primitive Technicolor. Thalberg was unhappy with the original staging of that number, finding it static and dull. He planned to film it again on a large stage with a moving staircase. Douglas Shearer (the brother of Norma), who was the head of the brand-new M-G-M sound department, suggested that the actors mime the second time around to avoid the expense of re-recording. This new technique was so successful that it was used from then on in most Hollywood musicals.

The gamble paid off, handsomely. The film grossed over $4,000,000 by the end of the year and won the Academy Award for Best Picture. Bessie Love was nominated for Best Actress of 1928/29 for her role in the film.

Another M-G-M film nominated for Best Picture that year was one of the first revue pictures. All the studios made these all-star extravaganzas, to show off the talents of their stars in the new medium of sound. Warner Bros. made *Show of Shows* (1929), and there was *Paramount on Parade* (1930) and the *Fox Follies of 1929*. But only M-G-M's *The Hollywood Revue of 1929* had John Gilbert and Norma Shearer playing the balcony scene from *Romeo and Juliet*, once seriously and a second time in twenties flapper slang for laughs. Also appearing were Jack Benny on the bass fiddle, Joan Crawford singing 'Got A Feelin' For You' and a trio of comedy stars, Marie Dressler, Bessie Love and Polly Moran with a new song by Arthur Freed and Nacio Herb Brown, called 'Singin' In The Rain.' It was a song that would be heard again on the M-G-M lot. It is of interest that the so-called 'white voice' of

John Gilbert recorded perfectly well on this occasion.

Another experiment with musical sound by M-G-M at this time was King Vidor's *Hallelujah* (1929). Vidor had long wanted to do a movie featuring black actors, but was given the go-ahead only when he offered to invest his own salary in the film because the head office feared it would be boycotted in the South. Vidor then had to find his cast, as there were few black actors in Hollywood at that time. When a black was called for, a white actor in the traditional minstrel black-face played the part. Even that stickler for accuracy, D W Griffith, had been forced to use white actors to play blacks in *Birth of*

a *Nation*. One of them was Elmo Lincoln, the screen's first Tarzan.

The story of *Hallelujah* concerned a young minister's wife (Nina Mae McKinney, late of the New York *Blackbirds* chorus) being tempted and saved by her husband who kills his rival. Vidor did location filming in Tennessee and added the sound track later at the studio. *Hallelujah* included many Negro spirituals and work songs ably performed by the Dixie Jubilee Singers, as well as two songs by Irving Berlin, 'Waitin' At The End Of The Road' and 'Swanee Shuffle.' The sound effects and camera work raise the film to a level with Vidor's other masterpieces, but it is sad to relate that the head office had been correct and very few Southern theaters chose to book *Hallelujah*. M-G-M would tread warily with black performers until it took a similar gamble with *Cabin In The Sky*, in 1942.

M-G-M was inclined to choose the first talking picture for their major stars with some care. Norma Shearer made the transition with *The Trial of Mary Dugan* (1929), a courtroom drama that had enjoyed a profitable run on Broadway. The studio even brought the lead, Raymond Hackett, west to repeat his role as the lawyer for the defense. Ramon Novarro appeared in *Devil May Care* (1929), an operetta set in Napoleonic France for his first speaking role, and Greta Garbo made *Anna Christie* (1929).

The dockside tragedy by Eugene O'Neill had not been Thalberg's initial choice for Garbo's first sound picture. He wanted the play *St Joan* by George Bernard Shaw. When

Shaw would not sell the rights, Thalberg thought about a remake of *The Passion of St Joan*, which had been made by the Danish director Carl Dreyer. Concerned that Garbo's accent would be a handicap at the box office, Thalberg decided to capitalize on it by making her play a Swede the first time out.

Such thinking might seem elementary, but several popular stars fell from grace when their voices proved radically different from their appearance. One was Reginald Owen, whose English accent did not jibe with the all-American boys he had been playing so successfully. Another was Constance Talmadge, who hailed from Brooklyn. Marion Davies revealed a slight stammer, while John Gilbert's normal speaking voice may have been sabotaged by early recording techniques.

The rights to *Anna Christie* were owned by First National Pictures, who had made a silent version of O'Neill's Pulitzer Prize-winner in 1923. Garbo turned it down at first because she felt that it portrayed the Swedes unfairly, but agreed to the film when Thalberg threatened to suspend her for breach of contract.

Anna Christie, adapted by Frances Marion, is the story of an ex-prostitute who returns home and is forced to reveal the sordidness of her life to her father and the Irishman who has fallen in love with her. It was a gamble for M-G-M to place their most glamorous star in such a grim feature. But Garbo's performance was electrifying. Equally good were George F Marion as the father, repeating the part he had played on

Broadway and in the 1923 silent version with Blanche Sweet, and Marie Dressler as the hard-drinking derelict, Marthy.

To produce films for the overseas market, Hollywood began making foreign language versions which were filmed at the same time. It is a curious fact that despite her dislike of the English language version of *Anna Christie*, directed by Clarence Brown, Garbo was very pleased with the German version shot at the same time, but directed by the Belgian Jacques Feyder, and considered it one of her finest films.

The film was advertised with the electrifying slogan: 'Garbo Talks!' and the audience was delighted with the film, from Garbo's first appearance and the immortal line, 'Gif me a viskey, ginger ale on the side, and don't be stingy, baby.'

M-G-M started another trend in 1930 with its production of the first prison movie, *The Big House*, starring Chester Morris and Robert Montgomery. Director George Hill scorned the superficial romanticism of Hollywood, and used naturalistic lighting and sound to enhance the performances of Wallace Beery as the brutish convict who controls the prisoners, Robert Montgomery, cast against type, as a tough kid who becomes a prison informer and Chester Morris as the basically good man who has paid for his one mistake.

Thalberg and the other members of the production staff had developed the habit by this time of previewing the new M-G-M films in Glendale or San Bernardino, and then making final cuts and alterations according to audience reaction. This was done with *The Big House* at an early stage, and Thalberg was surprised to discover that the audience had been apathetic to what was hoped to be one of the major productions of 1930. On Thalberg's orders certain scenes were reshot, turning the female lead (Leila Hyams) from one convict's wife into his sister, so that the subsequent romance between Hyams and the other convict (Chester Morris) was less threatening. Once again Thalberg was right. The audience loved the new version, and it returned a profit of some

$460,000. It also won Frances Marion the Academy Award for Best Writing and a new category, Best Sound Recording, was won by Douglas Shearer. (The French language version was filmed at the same time, and Charles Boyer made his M-G-M debut playing the part of the informer.) Soon after, the prison movie had become so popular that even Laurel and Hardy made one, *Pardon Us* (1931), shot on *The Big House* set.

Opposite: Anna Christie *(1930) starred Greta Garbo, with George F Marion as her father.*
Top right: Chester Morris and Wallace Beery in The Big House *(1930).*

Right: Pardon Us *(1931) was one of the first full-length Laurel and Hardy comedies.*

Another George Hill film was a surprise hit – *Min and Bill* (1930) – starring Wallace Beery and Marie Dressler. Adapted by Frances Marion from the novel *Dark Star* by Lorna Moon, it was the story of a dockside waif, adopted by an old couple who eventually accidentally kill the child's dissolute mother. Beery and Dressler played off one another beautifully, and Dressler especially had the opportunity to cover every emotion of which she was capable. Her performance won her the Academy Award for Best Actress for 1930/31, and her career, which had been on a downslide before *Anna Christie*, had turned around.

As with *The Big House*, George Hill had used his lighting and setting to advantage, and the dockyard slums of *Min and Bill* are as believable as the prison. Thalberg was so pleased with his stars that he planned to use them together in a variety of similar films, but the only one that actually developed was *Tugboat Annie* (1934).

Thalberg continued to experiment with the motion picture and sound. Remembering the success of earlier films shot in exotic locations, *White Shadows in the South Seas* (1928) and *The Pagan* (1929), Thalberg sent director W S 'One-shot Woody' Van Dyke to Africa, with a cast of three, Harry Carey, Duncan Renaldo and Edwina Booth, and a script patched together from the memoirs of 'a great white hunter,' known as 'Trader' Horn. After months of shooting, the company was recalled. As usual, Van Dyke had miles of film, but the scenario seemed to be missing.

With the addition of more animal footage, shot in Mexico and on the back lot, and more scenes of dialogue, made by superimposing studio action on the African footage, Thalberg ended up with an entertaining bit of nonsense about the great hunter whose companion falls in love with a white goddess who lives in the African jungle. *Trader Horn* became a surprise hit of 1931, and its success led M-G-M into negotiations for the Tarzan novels of Edgar Rice Burroughs.

Above left: *Wallace Beery and Marie Dressler confront one another in* Min and Bill *(1930).*
Left: *Harry Carey as the great white hunter* Trader Horn *(1931) with Duncan Renaldo and Edwina Booth.*

Opposite top: *Norma Shearer as Jan Ashe and Clark Gable as Ace Willfong in* A Free Soul *(1931).*

Trader Horn was the first of many movies to be made in Africa, but Van Dyke's lack of control also led to the establishment of the back lot, where the exotic settings could be duplicated, allowing rushes to be developed and seen, and expenses to be kept down.

In 1973, during the waning days of M-G-M, the movie was remade starring Rod Taylor. It too was shot in Africa, but that and the title were the only things the two films had in common. The original *Trader Horn* (1931) is still an exciting, if dated, adventure. Even the white goddess seems to belong. All that is lost with the remake.

One of the stock characters of the cinema in the thirties was the spoiled rich girl, and a prime M-G-M example was Norma Shearer in *A Free Soul* (1931). Based on a popular and successful stage play by Adela Rogers St John, the plot combined the popular gangster genre with a courtroom drama and threw in the spoiled rich girl as an added attraction.

What separates this film from many others like it were the performances. Norma Shearer played the heroine Jan Ashe as an intelligent girl, bored with the life society has created for her and attracted almost against her will to the wonderfully named Ace Willfong (Clark Gable), a gangster who was once a client of her father, an attorney (Lionel Barrymore). When Shearer realizes that Gable has been using her and that the escapades she had found amusing involve breaking the law, she attempts to leave him. They fight and Gable is killed by her scholarly fiancé, Leslie Howard. In a brilliant trial

scene, Barrymore defends Howard successfully, before he (Barrymore) drops dead in the courtroom. Sadder but wiser, Shearer returns to Howard, who was willing to give her the opportunity to discover her own mind and heart.

At this point in his career, Clark Gable was frequently cast as the villain. The familiar face, then without the mustache, has the sleek good looks that fit the scoundrel parts he played at that time. Even his rough handling of women seemed to attract fans, but his evident charm and sex appeal make his appeal to an intelligent girl like Miss Shearer more believable. Their love scenes, which are unusually aggressive on her part, are given an extra touch of scandal when the script indicates that she is his mistress.

The other triumphant performer was Lionel Barrymore as the father. An M-G-M player since *The Barrier* (1926), Barrymore's range of character parts was phenomenal. During the silent era, he played several villains, and also directed a number of films including *Madame X* (1929) with Ruth Chatterton, and *His Glorious Night* (1930), John Gilbert's first talkie. As the criminal lawyer, a father who is too busy to control his headstrong daughter, Barrymore was brilliant. The climactic courtroom scene was shot in a single take and his performance won Barrymore an Academy Award as Best Actor for 1930/31.

Throughout the early years of sound, Hollywood kept trying to entice established stars from Broadway to make movies, in the opinion that at least those people knew how to speak, which was still not always the case with an established

Above: *Lewis Stone as the doctor comforts Helen Hayes in* The Sin of Madelon Claudet *(1931).*
Opposite: *Alfred Lunt and Lynn Fontanne appeared in* The Guardsman *(1931), an adaptation of one of their great Broadway successes.*

Left: *Wallace Beery starred with Jackie Cooper in* The Champ *(1931).*

movie star. One of those who went West was Helen Hayes. Miss Hayes, who had made her theatrical debut at the age of five, had an ardent fan in Edgar Selwyn, who was now a writer-director at M-G-M and in charge of a project called *Lullaby*. It was a story of a young French girl, deceived in love, who bears a child and abandons the baby when she becomes a prostitute, but in the course of her trade avoids sailors because she knows her son is one. In an unusual turn of events, Miss Hayes' husband, screen writer Charles MacArthur, was allowed to see this turkey of a script about ten days before his wife arrived in Hollywood.

MacArthur set to work, and was still rewriting when the cast assembled in front of the camera. Among the alterations, besides the title change to *The Sin of Madelon Claudet* (1931), that made it more palatable was changing the son into a doctor, and making the necessity of raising the money for medical school the reason his mother turns to prostitution. Despite this, the picture was a disaster at the preview. Once again, Thalberg had the bright idea. He inserted a scene in the delivery room where the girl at first refuses to look at the child, and then is overcome with mother love. Another addition took place in the doctor's office, where the mother, unknown to her son, comes as a patient. She moves about, touching the various instruments, and eventually the doctor listens to her heartbeat with his head against her breast. It was mawkish, but Miss Hayes was one of the few actresses that could carry it off. She also carried off the Academy Award for Best Actress that year.

After the success of *The Big House* and *Min and Bill*, Wallace Beery, like his co-star, Marie Dressler, saw his career take a turn for the better. After a gangster film, *The Secret Six* (1931), his next movie was *The Champ* (1931), in which Beery played a down-and-out boxer opposite ten-year-old Jackie Cooper as his son. Directed by King Vidor, the film was shot in the less salubrious neighborhoods of Tia Juana, Mexico. The original screenplay by Frances Marion called for the old pugilist to make a comeback and die in defeat. After a depressing preview, Marion and Vidor agreed to have Beery win the fight before he died. The audience loved it, cried buckets over it, and *The Champ* became the top grossing film of 1931 for M-G-M. The picture, Vidor's direction and Marion's screenplay were all nominated for Academy Awards, but the only winner was the Champ himself, Wallace Beery, who won the Award for Best Actor.

Another attempt by Mayer and Thalberg to bring the luminaries of Broadway to Hollywood was the filming of Ferenc Molnár's comedy *The Guardsman* (1931) with Alfred Lunt and Lynn Fontanne, who had played it in New York. The story of the jealous actor who attempts to seduce his own wife while in disguise, was a critical hit and the Lunts acquitted themselves with honor in the new medium. But the play may have been too sophisticated for Middle America, and it was not a major success.

Thalberg's plans for filming more of the Lunts' hits, especially *Elizabeth the Queen*, a scene of which appears as a prologue to *The Guardsman*, and *Reunion In Vienna*, fell apart over contract negotiations. At least, *The Guardsman* has preserved one performance by two great actors in their prime.

Despite the lack of success in that genre, Thalberg still felt that it was possible to produce sophisticated films, and make them profitable. Perhaps the general public would enjoy such movies if their favorite stars were featured in them. Thalberg had just the right property, an adaptation of a German novel by Vicki Baum called *Menschen im Hotel*. As *Grand Hotel*, the play had been running in New York for over two years.

Grand Hotel (1932) was one of the first movies where a group of characters come together unexpectedly in a brief encounter that changes their lives. Following his original plan, Thalberg loaded the film with stars: two Barrymores, Wallace Beery, Joan Crawford and even Greta Garbo. This was not actually as extravagant as it might seem, since all the players were under contract and could be working on other films when not needed for *Grand Hotel*.

The plot of *Grand Hotel* is not really complicated. A penniless aristocrat turned jewel thief, Baron von Gaigern (John Barrymore) has established himself at the Grand Hotel in Berlin to steal the fabulous pearl necklace of the great dancer Grusinskaya (Garbo), but when he meets her they fall in love. Also in the hotel is an industrialist (Wallace Beery), who has hired a hotel stenographer (Joan Crawford) to take notes during an important business meeting. The fifth main character is the minor clerk (Lionel Barrymore) in Beery's company who is blowing his life savings at the hotel having learned that he has a terminal illness.

Meeting the clerk, Kringelein, at the hotel desk, where the staff is being dismissive to the old man in the shabby clothes with paper parcels instead of proper luggage, the Baron takes him on as a protegé. Together they meet the stenographer Flaemmchen, who instantly falls for the Baron. They are interrupted by the industrialist, von Preysing, who had his

eye on Flaemmchen for himself, and is at the end of his tether over a merger that will either save his business or allow it to go bankrupt. Flaemmchen, realizing that the Baron is no longer interested in her, decides to improve her lot by becoming von Preysing's mistress. Their assignation that night is interrupted by the Baron who has decided to rob von Preysing, since he cannot take Grusinskaya's necklace to pay off the gang that has advanced him money. The Baron and

Right: *Olga Baclanova is transformed from a beautiful trapeze artist into a monstrous sideshow attraction in* Freaks *(1932).*

Opposite top: *John Barrymore as Baron von Gaigern falls in love with Greta Garbo, the beautiful dancer Grusinskaya in* Grand Hotel *(1932).*

Opposite bottom: *The industrialist von Preysing (Wallace Beery) interrupts a mild flirtation between the stenographer Flaemmchen (Joan Crawford) and his old clerk Kringelein (Lionel Barrymore) in* Grand Hotel *(1932).*

von Preysing struggle and the Baron is killed. Flaemmchen runs to Kringelein for help, and eventually von Preysing is taken away by the police. Kringelein and Flaemmchen decide to go to Paris to seek medical aid, and poor Grusinskaya heads for her next booking in Vienna expecting to meet the Baron on the train, not knowing that he is dead.

The film opens and closes with Lewis Stone, as the hotel doctor, a scarred, somewhat cynical character remarking, 'Nothing ever happens at Grand Hotel.' Edmund Goulding directed this totally satisfying film, and gave it a strong European feeling, from the brilliant art-deco design of the hotel itself to the poignant shot where a broom sweeping in the hall the morning after the Baron's death is seen to negligently sweep away the Baron's adored small dachshund, as a member of the staff is told to 'get rid of it.' A less painful sequence is offered by the nervous tension of Jean Hersholt as the night porter awaiting the birth of his first child.

Over 50 years after its triumphant premiere, *Grand Hotel* still ranks as one of the most impressive of the early M-G-M films. That it won the Award as Best Picture of 1931/32 came as no surprise.

Not satisfied with his own triumphs, Thalberg thought to borrow ideas from other studios, and asked director Tod Browning to give him something that would 'out-horror' Universal's *Frankenstein.* Browning obliged with something so horrible that it was banned in England until 1963. This was

Freaks (1932), a real monster movie, set in a circus sideshow, and using actual sideshow freaks as its stars. The horror arises because it is the 'normal' characters, the trapeze artiste Cleopatra (Olga Baclanova) and the strong man Hercules (Henry Victor) who are monsters, cruel and unfeeling. The freaks are endearing and sympathetic as their lives behind the sideshow are revealed – their delight in the birth of a baby to the bearded lady and the ways that they overcome their various handicaps to lead normal lives. It is only when one of the midgets (Harry Earles) marries Cleopatra that the freaks as a group take on a menacing aspect. When they discover that she is poisoning him for his money, they take their revenge. In a truly frightening chase, because so little can be seen and so much is left to the imagination, the two lovers, Cleopatra and Hercules, are trapped by the freaks. He is emasculated and she becomes truly 'one of us' and is turned into a chicken woman, with no legs. The slow pan down into the pen in which she is displayed is one of the most horrific in all of movie history.

Despite the horror at the end, much of the audience sympathy remains with the freaks. But in its own time, the film was a terrible financial failure, and Tod Browning, who made such classics as *London After Midnight* (1927) and *Dracula* (1930), never again reached such a macabre height.

One M-G-M star who had not appeared in *Grand Hotel*, although the role of Baron von Gaigern had been intended for him, was John Gilbert. His career had never recovered

more's character, Prince Paul Chegodieff, was supposed to have joined in the plot to assassinate Rasputin because that monk had raped his fiancée. It was unfortunate that the disclaimer that ran before the film, suggested that 'A few of the characters are still alive.' Immediately, at least one of them made his presence known.

Prince Paul Yousepoff had never made a secret of the fact that he had been among those who lured Rasputin to his death. However, the prince took a very dim view of anybody libeling his wife. Two law suits arose, one in New York and one in London. The English suit was settled quite quickly in favor of the Yousepoffs. M-G-M appealed, but lost. The disclaimer and the scene of Princess 'Natasha's rape' were cut, and M-G-M paid out a total of almost $250,000. This is one of the reasons that most movies today carry the lines:

The events and characters in this film are fictional and any resemblance to characters living or dead is purely coincidental.

For the record, Tsar Nicholas was played by Ralph Morgan, the Tsarevitch by Tad Alexander, a precursor of Freddie Bartholomew, and Diana Wynyard played the possibly raped fiancée of Prince Chegodieff. The Yousepoffs lived to a placid and comfortable old age.

After the success of *Trader Horn*, M-G-M bought the rights to the Tarzan stories of Edgar Rice Burroughs. It was not an

from his early difficulties with sound recording, and he dispaired of M-G-M finding him a vehicle that would allow him to show his undisputed talents. Irving Thalberg came to his rescue by reviving a plot that Gilbert himself had written some four years earlier, a rather cynical comedy about the household staff of an aristocratic Viennese household.

Gilbert had the part of the unscrupulous and lecherous chauffeur, a part so unsympathetic that Thalberg would never have let him take it when his popularity had been at its height. In *Downstairs* (1932), Gilbert at last had the opportunity to move away from the great-lover parts that had in one sense ruined him. His costars were Reginald Owen and Olga Baclanova as the Baron and Baroness, and a young ingenue named Virginia Bruce played Gilbert's love interest, the maid Anna. Her other suitor was the butler, Paul Lukas. It would be nice to report that *Downstairs* was an unqualified success, however, though Gilbert had always wanted to play character parts, his fans still wanted the romantic hero. The one happy outcome of the film was Gilbert's marriage to Virginia Bruce. For what it is worth, posterity can acknowledge that Gilbert's voice records perfectly.

Having starred two Barrymores in *Grand Hotel*, Thalberg thought that three would bring even greater success, but finding a screenplay that would use their talents to the full was more difficult. Eventually the studio settled on a re-working of one aspect of the Russian Revolution, the influence of the monk Rasputin on the Russian Imperial family. Lionel's hystrionics were deemed suitable for Rasputin, Ethel was cast as the Tsarina Alexandra, and John as 'Prince Paul Chegodieff,' one of the assassins of the mad monk.

The publicity office had hoped for family infighting to publicize *Rasputin and the Empress* (1932) but in this respect the Barrymores, being professionals, let them down. Ethel in particular was more interested that the major characters, whom she had known, were treated fairly than anything else. The fireworks came after the film was released. John Barry-

Opposite top: *The chauffeur (John Gilbert) begins his seduction of the virtuous maid, Anna (Virginia Bruce) in* Downstairs *(1932).*
Opposite below: *The monk Rasputin (Lionel Barrymore) prays for the recovery of the Tsarevitch (Tad Alexander) who is held by his mother the Empress Alexandra (Ethel Barrymore) in* Rasputin and the Empress *(1932). John Barrymore as Prince Chegodieff is at the left, and Ralph Morgan as the Tsar stands behind.*

Right: *Johnny Weismuller as* Tarzan The Ape Man *(1932) with Jane (Maureen O'Sullivan) and Cheetah.*
Below: *Clark Gable as the plantation manager Dennis Carson informs Vantine (Jean Harlow) that she will have to leave –* Red Dust *(1932).*

original decision. The first Tarzan movie had been made in 1918, with Elmo Lincoln in a lion-skin tunic and headband. Thalberg's idea of Tarzan was somewhat different from his creator, more illiterate and simple, less of an instinctive gentleman, and Thalberg had the perfect player in mind.

Johnny Weismuller had been an Olympic swimmer, winning no fewer than five gold medals in the 1924 and 1928 Olympics. His championship technique on the rings came in handy for the jungle vine sequences. His true love Jane, the orphaned daughter of an English trader, was played by Maureen O'Sullivan.

Tarzan The Ape Man (1932) concerned an expedition to the famed elephant burial grounds by Jane's father, who is soon killed. She is rescued by Tarzan, and won over by his simple nature. Her previous suitor recognizes defeat and returns to England. The screenplay was by Cyril Hume, though Ivor Novello is said to have been responsible for the famous 'Tarzan-Jane' dialogue.

Sparing no expense, M-G-M shot part of the series in Malibu, a full 20 miles from Los Angeles, and Woody Van Dyke, who had previously made *White Shadows in the South Seas* and *Trader Horn*, was the director. The new series was a bonanza for all concerned. Weismuller stayed at M-G-M to make five more, and some eight or nine Tarzans later he is still the best-remembered. Part of his fame may be due to the famous yell, which was created by Douglas Shearer, electronically embellished and run backwards.

Another hit of 1932 shot in the jungle was *Red Dust*, starring Clark Gable, Mary Astor and Jean Harlow, though this time the jungle was supposed to be Indochina. Gable played Dennis Carson, the manager of a rubber plantation, whose life is disrupted first by the appearance of Vantine (Jean Harlow), a prostitute on the run from the police, and later by Barbara (Mary Astor), the wife of a fever-stricken engineer (Gene Raymond). Vantine returns, and finds that Carson has fallen in love with Barbara. While Willis (Raymond) is in the

jungle, Barbara and Carson become lovers, but Carson tries to break off the affair when Willis returns. Barbara shoots Carson in a jealous rage, but Vantine tells Willis that Barbara was only protecting herself from Carson's advances. Willis and Barbara leave, and Vantine and Carson realize that they are meant for one another.

The teamwork between Gable and Harlow was a delight to behold, and appreciated by even the most stuffy critics. As the icy wife who also falls for Gable, Mary Astor was superb. The supporting cast of Gene Raymond, Tully Marshall and Donald Crisp deserve praise as well, and the direction by Victor Fleming runs neatly between comedy and drama.

In 1933, Irving Thalberg took an extended leave of absence for the sake of his health, and Mayer brought his son-in-law, David O Selznick, into the studio. Another newcomer who joined the ranks of the M-G-M directors at that time was George Cukor, who had previously been working at R-K-O. As their first joint project, Selznick and Cukor chose an adaptation of the Broadway hit by George S Kaufman and Edna Ferber, *Dinner At Eight*.

It has been said that *Dinner at Eight* (1933) is one of the occasions when Hollywood improved on the original. Certainly the cast was outstanding. The host and hostess were played by Lionel Barrymore and Billie Burke, and their guests, whose subplots all entwined, include Wallace Beery and Jean Harlow as the *nouveau riche* tycoon and his brash young wife, Marie Dressler as an aging actress and John Barrymore as an aging actor who has fallen in love with his host's young daughter, Madge Evans.

Cukor introduces his characters as they prepare for the dinner party that night, and the audience is allowed to see the deceptions and machinations that are common to them all. The real stand-out performance is Miss Dressler's, especially in the scene in which she comforts Madge Evans after John Barrymore commits suicide. Harlow and Beery are delightful as the vulgar couple on the make.

Another M-G-M star who had been moving from strength to strength was Joan Crawford, and *Dancing Lady* (1933) was one of her biggest hits. In it she played an aspiring young dancer who manages to climb from burlesque to Broadway, and end up with the right man, the dance director, Clark Gable, rather than the rich playboy, Franchot Tone, who tried to sabotage her show in order to marry her. It also featured Fred Astaire in his movie debut as Miss Crawford's partner in a number called 'Rhythm of the Day,' but the best song was by Rodgers and Hart, 'Everything I Have Is Yours.'

Since *Grand Hotel*, Garbo had made only one film, the strange adaptation of Pirandello's *As You Desire Me* (1932), with Erich von Stroheim, and there were rumors that she had retired back to Sweden. On the contrary, M-G-M had been looking for another solid part for her. What they came up with was *Queen Christina* (1933), a romantization of the life of one of the monarchs of seventeenth-century Sweden.

Her co-star was John Gilbert, for Garbo herself had asked Mayer to let him play the part of the Spanish Ambassador who became the queen's lover, over the young Englishman who had been signed for the role, Laurence Olivier. Olivier himself recalls that he was so in awe of Garbo that his performance was impossible. The old radiance between the two stars was somewhat dimmed, except in the scene at the inn, where she moves about touching various articles, 'memorizing this room in which I have been so happy.' The director Rouben Mamoulian may have borrowed the idea from *The Sin of Madelon Claudet*, but it still stands out as an unforgettable piece of movie magic. The other image that is impossible to forget is the scene at the end, where she stands in the prow of a ship with the wind blowing in her face. (If she is to get anywhere, it is hoped that the wind is blowing into the sails from behind as well.) The expression on her face allows the audience to read many things into it. The director achieved it by asking his star to think of nothing.

Though *Queen Christina* was a great success for M-G-M and Garbo, it was the end for Gilbert. Once again Mayer's animosity proved too strong. Gilbert would not make another movie for a year, and that one, *The Captain Hates The Sea* (1935), for Columbia was his last. He died just over a year after its release of heart failure. He was thirty-eight.

Right: *John Gilbert costarred with Greta Garbo for the last time in* Queen Christina *(1933).*

Opposite top: *Joan Crawford played a musical star on the rise in* Dancing Lady *(1933). Fred Astaire played himself.*
Opposite below: *Billie Burke, the hostess, and Marie Dressler, one of her guests, in* Dinner at Eight *(1933).*

THE GOLDEN AGE

IN 1934, M-G-M WAS TEN years old, and Mayer and the Loew's Inc. office could certainly look back with pride at a decade of accomplishment. The studio had the highest number of hits, and the highest profits of any of the eight major companies. The new studio had been able to weather both the onset of sound and the Depression without missing a beat. M-G-M had made its mark with musicals, comedies and dramas, and its roster of talent continued to increase.

The studio opened its second decade with a remake of one of its silent hits, *The Merry Widow* (1934), but the stars and director were new acquisitions from Paramount. Jeanette MacDonald, Maurice Chevalier and Ernst Lubitsch had made a series of very successful musicals at the other studio, including *The Love Parade* (1929) and *One Hour With You* (1932). Lubitsch's idea of Vienna was more in line with Franz Lehar's, and he had the advantage of two good singers in MacDonald and Chevalier. It is said that Joan Crawford, among others, begged to play the glamorous widow, and it is a matter of record that Metropolitan Opera star Grace Moore was also under consideration.

The result was one of the best musicals of all time. With Chevalier, MacDonald displayed a wonderful sexy sense of humor and the M-G-M studios gave the sets and costumes the opulence the music demanded. The lyrics to Lehar's beautiful score were rewritten by Richard Rodgers, Lorenz Hart and Gus Kahn.

The operetta is complete with all the little gags that help make up the 'Lubitsch Touch.' In one, Edward Everett Horton, as the ambassador in Paris, consults his code book on receiving a letter beginning with the word 'Darling.' This translates as 'Of all the idiots in the diplomatic service, you are the worst.' Lubitsch also used imaginative camera angles and lighting to cleverly heighten the atmosphere in many of the musical numbers.

The Merry Widow was certainly not the only musical by Lehar made by M-G-M. *Gypsy Love* had become *The Rogue Song* (1929) starring Lawrence Tibbett, with Laurel and Hardy. In 1933, Laurel and Hardy turned on opera again and filmed an adaptation of Daniel François Auber's *Fra*

Diavolo, which starred Dennis King, but became a vehicle for Stan and Ollie's gags. In 1934, they gave the same treatment to Victor Herbert's *Babes in Toyland*.

As two fumbling toymakers, Stannie Dum and Ollie Dee, they build 100 six-foot toy soldiers instead of 600 1-foot toy soldiers. This catastrophe means that they don't dare ask the Toymaker for an advance so that their landlady Widow Peep, The Old Woman Who Lives In A Shoe, will not be dispossessed of her shoe by the villain, Barnaby, who is willing to marry Bo-Peep as payment. To allow Bo-Peep to elope with Tom-Tom (The Piper's Son), Stan is dressed up as the bride. When the elopement is discovered, Tom-Tom is exiled to Bogeyland. When the Bogeys, who are such things as nightmares are made of, storm the walls of Toyland, Stan and Ollie set their six-foot toy soldiers to repulse them and Toyland is saved.

It was a delightfully silly piece of nonsense, though minus most of Herbert's score, which hit a chord at the time, being considered suitable for children, and has been re-released many times, frequently under the title of *The Parade Of The Wooden Soldiers*. In 1935, Laurel and Hardy would make the last of their operatic spoofs for Hal Roach and M-G-M, *The Bohemian Girl* by Michael Balfe.

After the success of *Dinner At Eight*, David O Selznick began work on *Viva Villa* (1934), the story of the Mexican bandit, Pancho Villa, with Wallace Beery in the lead role. M-G-M wanted to film on location and entered into some rather delicate negotiations with the Mexican Government. These were aggravated by elements in the government who wanted Villa portrayed as an arrogant, mindless peon. Director Howard Hawks had begun shooting the exteriors before the Ben Hecht script was approved.

Government co-operation vanished when actor Lee Tracy, after a night's drinking, managed to urinate on a military parade passing beneath his hotel window in Mexico City. The company returned to the Culver City lot to complete shooting, Tracy was replaced by Stuart Erwin, and Jack Conway took over the direction from Howard Hawks.

No matter who was responsible, *Viva Villa* is an extra-

Above: *Joseph Schildkraut as Pascal and Wallace Beery as Pancho Villa in* Viva Villa! *(1934).*
Right: *Stan Laurel and Oliver Hardy load a toy cannon to repel the Bogeymen in* Babes in Toyland *(1934).*
Previous spread: *Dorothy (Judy Garland), the Tin Woodman (Jack Haley, the Cowardly Lion (Bert Lahr) and the Scarecrow (Ray Bolger) approach the Castle of the Wicked Witch of the West in* The Wizard of Oz *(1939).*

Opposite: *Jeanette MacDonald as the glamorous widow and Maurice Chevalier as Prince Danilo in* The Merry Widow *(1934).*

ordinary film. Part of the credit goes to Beery, whose portrait of Pancho runs from a simple romantic to an intense patriot with a maniacal side when angry. But the visual aspects of the film are also overwhelming. The directors placed their characters in the landscape in a fashion similar to European directors, such as Sergei Eisenstein. It is still a very powerful film.

A complete contrast was *The Thin Man* (1934), a fast paced murder mystery. Based on Dashiell Hammett's detective novel, the film starred William Powell and Myrna Loy as crime-solvers Nick and Nora Charles. The continuing popularity of this movie is probably due to the interplay between the stars. Movie audiences who had grown used to seeing marriage portrayed on the screen as an ordeal, were enchanted with the open affection and wisecracking relationship of Powell and Miss Loy. The stars had been paired earlier in *Manhattan Melodrama* (1934), and it was the success of that film which led Mayer to agree to cast them in *The Thin Man*.

The murder of 'the thin man' takes place before the audience is introduced to Nick and Nora, but from the first scene with William Powell, where he explains to a bartender that a martini must be shaken in waltz time, the pace changes and the audience is hooked. The movies (there were eventually six of them) are notable for the sheer amount of alcohol that is consumed in them. It has been suggested that the writers, Frances Goodrich and Albert Hackett, were celebrating the end of prohibition by allowing the entire cast of characters to drink to excess. The series also made a star out of Asta, the wire-haired terrier.

Originally planned as a 'B' picture, and shot by Woody Van

Dyke in only two weeks, the film stunned the studio with its popularity. It grossed $2,000,000 in its first year and was honored with five Academy Award nominations.

Thalberg at this time was involved with *The Barretts of Wimpole Street* (1934), a play by Rudolph Besier, which had been a great Broadway hit with Katherine Cornell and Brian Aherne. Thalberg believed that the role of the invalid poet, Elizabeth Barrett, would be perfect for his wife, Norma Shearer. Unfortunately William Randolph Hearst felt it was the proper part for Marion Davies, since he always had thought she should appear in serious dramatic roles rather than the light comedies which were really her strength. Davies even made a screen test, but Mayer sided with Thalberg. He knew this would be a big-budget picture, and Davies' films were not the money-spinners they had been.

Hearst agreed reluctantly but his papers carried no publicity for *The Barretts of Wimpole Street* while it was being filmed. Miss Shearer's costars included Fredric March as Robert Browning and Charles Laughton as Elizabeth's father, Edward Moulton Barrett. The film was directed by Sidney Franklin, and the camerawork by William Daniels contributed to the glory of the film. Miss Shearer was never better, but it was Laughton as the tyrannical father, whose love for his eldest daughter may border on the incestuous, who really deserved a nomination. Richard Watts in the New York *Herald Tribune* agreed. 'The screen has been handsomely loyal to the play . . . [Laughton's] portrayal of the stern, repressed family tyrant is nothing short of a masterpiece of power and understanding and sheer dramatic art.'

In 1956, M-G-M would remake the film with Jennifer Jones, Bill Travers and John Gielgud. Sidney Franklin again direc-

Opposite: *William Powell and Myrna Loy starred as Nick and Nora Charles in* The Thin Man *(1934). Asta played Asta.*
Right: *Jackie Cooper and Wallace Beery costarred again as Jim Hawkins and Long John Silver in* Treasure Island *(1934).*

Below: *Norma Shearer as the invalid poet Elizabeth Barrett is carried upstairs by her irate father, played by Charles Laughton, while Fredric March as her suitor Robert Browning looks on –* The Barretts of Wimpole Street *(1934).*

ted, but the magic was missing. Perhaps the less flamboyant acting of the fifties was less suitable to a play written in the thirties.

Another M-G-M triumph of 1934 was the first adaptation of Robert Louis Stevenson's tale of piracy, *Treasure Island*. Director Victor Fleming, who was becoming *the* M-G-M director for adventure pictures, created a faithful and straightforward movie, starring Jackie Cooper as Jim Hawkins and Wallace Beery as Long John Silver. Beery's performance may be a bit overdone, but the supporting cast of Otto Kruger as Doctor Livesey, Lewis Stone as Captain Smollett, Nigel Bruce as Squire Trelawney and Lionel Barrymore as Billy Bones, cannot be faulted.

From the first creaking of the inn sign at the Admiral Benbow Inn, where Jim Hawkins, the son of the owner, works as a pot boy, to the return of the *Hispaniola* laden with treasure and Long John Silver in irons, the picture doesn't flag. This may be in part due to the script by John Lee Mahin, but also owes a great deal to the impressive camerawork of Ray June and Clyde DeVinna.

Another great English classic was being filmed on the M-G-M lot at the same time, David O Selznick's production of *David Copperfield* (1934). Once again Selznick had gone for an all-star cast, including Basil Rathbone as a truly frightening Mr Murdstone and Edna May Oliver as the ultimate Aunt Betsey Trotwood. Much of the film depends on the performance of the child David. Mayer had originally wanted to cast Jackie Cooper in the role, but Selznick held out for the child he and director George Cukor had discovered while hunting locations in England. Thus Freddie Bartholomew joined the M-G-M stock company. Two other unusual pieces of casting can be found in *David Copperfield*, Roland Young as Uriah Heep, and W C Fields as Mr Micawber. Fields replaced Charles Laughton, who recognized that he was wrong for the part.

The location hunting that Selznick and Cukor had done in England was wasted. Cedric Gibbons, the M-G-M Art Director, built a nineteenth century England at Malibu and on the back lot, using points of detail in the novel in an almost claustrophobic fashion. The screenplay by Howard Estabrook and Hugh Walpole preserves much of the humor and most of the characters of Dicken's sprawling novel.

The Marx Brothers made their first movie, *The Cocoanuts* (1929) at the old Paramount studios in Astoria, Long Island. At the time, they were also appearing on Broadway in *Animal Crackers*. After its run, this too was filmed by Paramount in 1930. Then they moved to Hollywood.

By 1934, their five-picture contract with Paramount had expired, and their latest film, *Duck Soup* (1933), had not been an unqualified success. Fortunately for posterity, Chico Marx played bridge with Irving Thalberg, and shortly thereafter the Marx Brothers were under contract to M-G-M.

Their first picture for the new studio was *A Night at the Opera* (1935). Thalberg took his production duties very seriously with the Marx Brothers, trying to recognize why the later films had not been successful. He hired Morris Ryskind

and George S Kaufman, who were responsible for *Animal Crackers* and *The Cocoanuts*, to write the screenplay. Thalberg also sent the Brothers out on the vaudeville circuit to try out several of the big scenes before a live audience. He gave them a good supporting cast, including the redoubtable Margaret Dumont.

One of the changes that Thalberg inserted was romantic interest, apart from Harpo's girl-chasing and Groucho's never-flagging interest in Margaret Dumont. In *A Night at the Opera* (1935) this is provided by Kitty Carlisle and Allan Jones as the young soprano and tenor who hope to sing at the Metropolitan. The plot also concerned a social-climbing dowager (Dumont) who has been assured by Groucho that she can get into society by investing $200,000 in the New York Opera. He introduces her to the opera director (Sig Rumann) who kisses her hand. (Groucho, of course, inspects the hand to make sure all her rings are still there.) After an ocean voyage back to New York, so that Groucho can squeeze the entire cast into the world's smallest stateroom, it is opening night. The boys sabotage the star tenor, so that the understudy tenor (Allan Jones) managed by Chico can take over. There is a lot of lovely mayhem during the performance when the opera changes with every scene shift.

A Night at the Opera was followed by *A Day at the Races* (1937), but by that time, Thalberg was dead, and no one was

Left: *W C Fields as Mr Micawber meets young David (Freddie Bartholomew) in* David Copperfield *(1934).*

Opposite top: *The stateroom scene from* A Night at the Opera *(1936), the first Marx Brothers movie produced by M-G-M.*
Opposite below: *Eleanor Powell was the dancing star of* Broadway Melody of 1936 *(1935).*

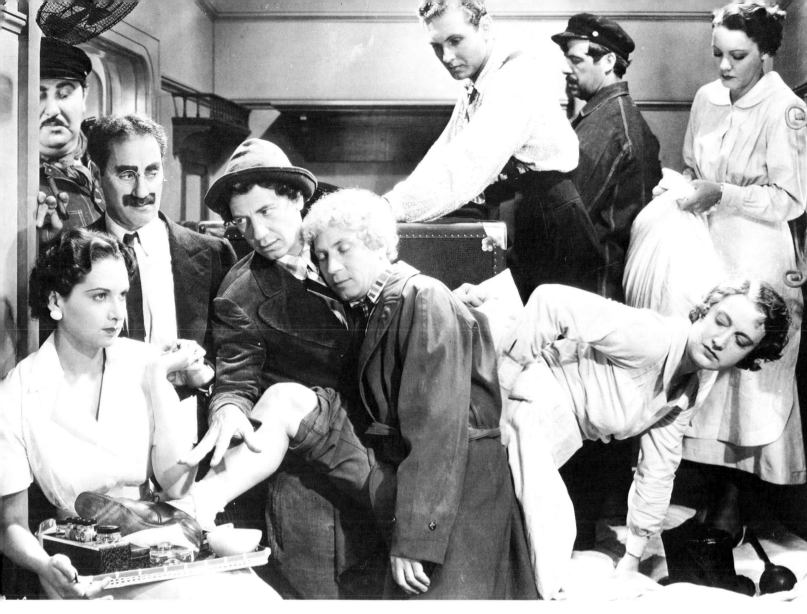

willing or able to take control. The Marx Brothers made two
more movies for M-G-M, each less successful than the last,
two for United Artists and then retired.

While established stars were being brought into the
studio, young talent was also being showcased. Among the
most popular of these was Eleanor Powell, who made her
debut in *Broadway Melody of 1936* (1935). This was not a
sequel to the 1928 blockbuster but had a brand new score
(except for the title song) and a brand new story about a
Broadway producer (Robert Taylor) torn between the
untalented woman who is rich enough to back his show
providing she gets the lead (June Knight), and his hometown
girlfriend (Miss Powell), whose theatrical ambitions he
doesn't take seriously until she pretends to be a French
chanteuse. Besides Miss Powell's dancing, the film is notable
for Robert Taylor's halting rendition of 'I've Got A Feelin'
You're Foolin'.' Other hits included 'You Are My Lucky Star'
and 'Broadway Rhythm.'

Following *The Merry Widow*, Jeanette MacDonald was cast
in an adaptation of another operetta, *Naughty Marietta*
(1935), by Victor Herbert. Her co-star was Nelson Eddy, an
M-G-M contract player since 1933, who had appeared in only
three movies in that time. His acting may have been a trifle
wooden, but his baritone voice blended perfectly with
MacDonald's soprano. The plot of *Naughty Marietta* involved
pirates, slaves and casket girls in old Louisiana, as well as a
French princess who has come to the new world to escape an
unwanted marriage. But since it also had songs like 'I'm
Falling In Love With Someone,' ''Neath the Southern Moon'

47

and 'Ah, Sweet Mystery of Life,' no one, least of all the public, seemed to care that the plot hadn't been original even in 1910.

'The Singing Sweethearts,' as they were dubbed, became the newest star team at M-G-M, who immediately put them into another operetta, Rudolph Friml's *Rose Marie* (1935).

This time M-G-M knew they had a winner, and producer Hunt Stromberg and director Woody Van Dyke were given a bigger budget. This allowed them to include the big production number 'Totem Tom-Tom,' which was shot at Lake Tahoe, and several operatic episodes. These were included because the heroine, Marie de Flor (MacDonald), was an opera singer who goes to the wilds of Canada to find her brother, who is up there somewhere having escaped from jail. She meets the Mountie who is tracking her brother, Sergeant Bruce (Eddy), and since the Mounties always get their man, he does, and the girl, too. Somehow they find time to sing 'The Song of the Mounties,' 'Indian Love Call' and 'Rose Marie, I Love You.'

Once again, MacDonald and Eddy had a triumph. So did the young actor who played the brother, James Stewart. *Rose Marie* was Stewart's second film. His previous one had been *The Murder Man* (1935) with Spencer Tracy.

By this time Selznick was again busy with another glossy adaptation of the classics. M-G-M had filmed a silent version of Tolstoy's *Anna Karenina* in 1927, with Greta Garbo and

Right: *Basil Rathbone (left) with Greta Garbo and Freddie Bartholomew in* Anna Karenina *(1935).*

Opposite top: *The Singing Sweethearts', Nelson Eddy and Jeanette MacDonald in their first M-G-M hit,* Naughty Marietta *(1935).*
Opposite bottom: *In* Rose Marie *(1935), MacDonald played an opera singer and Eddy a Canadian Mountie.*

John Gilbert, under the title of *Love.* Now Selznick was ready to do it again, with authentic costumes, relying more on the original story and less on the attachment between the stars.

Garbo was once again cast as Anna and her costars were Fredric March as Vronsky and Basil Rathbone, at his best, as her cold and stuffy husband Karenin. Freddie Batholomew had the important, though brief, role of Anna's son Sergei. Again the story centered on the romance of Anna and Vronsky, contrasting the stern manner of Karenin with the ardor of the young officer. Garbo is swept into the affair almost against her will. When she does go away with Vronsky, she has burned her bridges. In time, Vronsky yearns to return to his life in the army and leaves Anna. She tries to reconcile with him before he leaves for service in the Turkish-Serbian War, but their meeting at the station is interrupted by his mother and the young woman Countess Vronsky hopes her son will marry. Reminded of the old railway worker who was killed under the wheels of a train at the time Anna and Vronsky met, Anna throws herself beneath the train.

The production values of the film are extremely high. Director Clarence Brown and cameraman William Daniels, who had also worked on *Love,* gave their new films all the pomp and ceremony that a movie set in pre-revolutionary Russia demanded, including incidental music by the Russian Symphony Choir. The memorable sound work included an ominous, perhaps amplified, tapping of the railway carriages'

wheels in all the scenes shot in the station. Despite the polish, many of the reviews were not favorable, finding the picture oppressive, and Garbo's performance too restrained, but it is a movie that is not easily forgotten.

Selznick was also involved with the first sound filming of Charles Dickens' *A Tale of Two Cities* (1935). It was a project Selznick felt very close to, for he himself had worked on the first draft of the screenplay with Donald Ogden Stewart. Ronald Colman was cast as Sydney Carton, the self-sacrificing hero, and Donald Woods as Charles Darnay. Selznick had toyed with the idea of having Colman play both parts until his star pointed out that in he first place, according to Dickens, Carton and Darnay merely resembled one another, and secondly, he wouldn't do it.

The vast set for the Bastille was constructed on the M-G-M back lot, to supplement the backdrop photography that Selznick had shot in France and England. The actual revolutionary episodes Selznick entrusted to Val Lewton and Jacques Tourneur, who would later become accomplished directors of horror movies.

Once again Selznick managed to capture the essence of Dickens without discarding too much of the characterization. Actually this was an easy task, because *A Tale Of Two Cities* is much more straightforward than *David Copperfield.* The cast was filled out by Elizabeth Allan as Lucie, Henry B Wathall as Dr Manette and Basil Rathbone as the Marquis de St Evremonde. Blanche Yurka knitted away as Madame Defarge and Edna May Oliver was formidable as Prossy, Lucie's maid.

Colman gave a restrained and very moving performance as Carton, and was especially memorable in the scene at Christmas time, watching the carollers and churchgoers on their way home, knowing he has none himself. His other triumph is, of course, the scene at the guillotine where he comforts the little seamstress (Isobel Jewell) who is ahead of him in line. Blessed with a beautifully articulate voice, Colman took all the cliché out of the familiar closing words.

For his final production of 1935, Irving Thalberg was working on *Mutiny on the Bounty*, based on the three novels of Charles Nordhoff and James Norman Hall and the actual log of Captain Bligh. Mayer was unhappy with the idea, since he didn't believe a mutineer could be the hero. Thalberg, on the other hand, saw Fletcher Christian as a man forced to follow his conscience for the good of his fellow-men. He felt it would be a perfect role for Clark Gable. Gable didn't think so, since he disliked playing in costume pictures, and this one would force him to shave off his mustache. Thalberg finally got him to agree, promising that if 'this one isn't one of

your greatest successes, I'll never ask you again to play a part you don't want to do.'

For Captain Bligh, Thalberg cast Charles Laughton, knowing that he would have the necessary presence, and that his part in *The Barretts of Wimpole Street* had made him familiar to the movie-going public. Franchot Tone was cast as Midshipman Byam.

While the film was in production, M-G-M acquired the rights to an Australian semi-documentary called *In the Wake of the Bounty*, partly to keep it out of the American theaters until their own film was finished. Thalberg also used some of the footage to make a short feature called *Pitcairn Island Today* to awaken interest in the audiences who may not have been aware of the story of the *Bounty*. (The actor who played Fletcher Christian in the Australian film was Errol Flynn.)

M-G-M's *Mutiny on the Bounty* (1935) sticks quite close to the historical record, only increasing the malevolence of Captain Bligh, which gave Charles Laughton a truly magnificent character to play. The film has its great strength in the scenes on shipboard as the tension among the crew builds, while the interlude in Tahiti is charming and idyllic. The

Opposite: *Ronald Colman (r) in* A Tale of Two Cities *(1935).*
Above: *Clark Gable and Charles Laughton in* Mutiny on the Bounty *(1935).*
Right: *William Powell and Myrna Loy in* The Great Ziegfeld *(1936).*

public loved it, and the film won the Academy Award for Best Picture, while all three of the leads were nominated for best actor. It is still the best of the *Mutiny* movies made to date.

The most expensive and longest film made by M-G-M to that time opened in 1936. This was *The Great Ziegfeld*, billed as a biography of the producer of the Follies, Florenz Ziegfeld, but actually a good way of hanging together a number of extravagant musical numbers, which included 'Rhapsody in Blue' and 'A Pretty Girl Is Like A Melody.' William Powell starred as Ziegfeld, with Luise Rainer as his first wife, Anna Held, and Myrna Loy as his second wife, Billie Burke. Rainer won the Academy Award as Best Actress, probably for the poignant scene in which she calls him on the telephone having heard about his remarriage. The film itself was also honored as Best Picture of the Year.

Above: *Eleanor Powell in the extravagant finale of* Born to Dance *(1936), 'Swingin' The Jinx Away.'*
Left: Wife versus Secretary *(1936) starred Jean Harlow, Clark Gable and Myrna Loy, here with May Robson.*

Opposite: *Leslie Howard and Norma Shearer starred in* Romeo and Juliet *(1936).*

Another musical of 1936 was *Born to Dance*, starring Eleanor Powell as the understudy of a review star, who naturally ends up playing the part. Her costars were Buddy Ebsen, James Stewart (who sang Cole Porter's 'Easy to Love' to her) and Una Merkel. Other Cole Porter numbers included 'I've Got You Under My Skin' and 'Swingin' The Jinx Away,' the big finale which had Miss Powell tapping all over the deck of a battleship.

After *Mutiny on the Bounty*, Gable regrew his mustache and costarred in a charming comedy with Myrna Loy and Jean Harlow called *Wife versus Secretary* (1936). Gable played a young publisher who sends for his secretary (Harlow) while on an overnight business trip to Havana. When Myrna Loy, his wife, hears of it, she prepares to take the next boat to Europe, until Harlow explains that that way she will lose her husband. James Stewart and May Robson were also featured. It was not an important movie, but it was well-played, especially by Harlow, who was reviewed as being 'so straight-forward and human and pleasant to observe.' It was also typical of the well-produced comedies that M-G-M was famous for at this time.

With the success of *Mutiny* assured, Thalberg turned to another pet project, *Romeo and Juliet* (1936). Once again Mayer was aghast, being well aware of the expense involved and the fact that the Warner Bros. production of Shakespeare's *A Midsummer Night's Dream* directed by Max Reinhardt had been a critical and box office failure. However, he was overridden by Thalberg and the New York office, which had the last word.

As expected, Thalberg spared no expense on the production. The main square of Verona was rebuilt on the back lot. The settings, costumes and some of the action were based on paintings by masters of the Early Italian Renaissance. The dances were choreographed by Agnes de Mille (regrettably most of them ended up on the cutting room floor) and director George Cukor gave full rein to bringing the poetry of description into action.

The cast was headed by Norma Shearer as Juliet. Shearer had wanted to play the part since she had camped it up with John Gilbert for *The Hollywood Revue*, and took great pains with the role, studying under such Shakespearean actresses as Constance Collier and Margaret Carrington.

The part of Romeo was first offered to Fredric March, although the gossip columns suggested that Gable was under

Left: *Jack Holt was Clark Gable's rival for Jeanette MacDonald in* San Francisco *(1936).*
Opposite: *Robert Taylor as Armand embraces Greta Garbo as the dying Marguerite in* Camille *(1936).*

Below: *The duel between Tybalt (John Barrymore, left) and Mercutio (Basil Rathbone) was a high point of* Romeo and Juliet *(1936).*

consideration. March declined, and the part went to Leslie Howard, who felt he was too old but eventually accepted.

Age was a problem with the entire cast. Shearer was 35, not 14, Howard was 42. However, since no less an authority than Ellen Terry has said 'an actress cannot play Juliet until she is too old to look like Juliet,' Thalberg was following a well-established precedent.

Others in the cast included Basil Rathbone as Tybalt and John Barrymore as Mercutio, whose duel and death scene is a high point of the film. However, Howard and Shearer both acquitted themselves with honor. Shearer actually did the potion scene in a single take, and the scene was also a one-shot without a cut. The public did not take to it as Thalberg had hoped, but the prestige value was enormous, and some people still regard it to be one of the best *Romeo and Juliet*s on screen.

Gable may not have played Romeo but he was much better occupied as Blackie Norton in *San Francisco* (1936). His costars were Jeanette MacDonald and Spencer Tracy, playing a priest for the first, but not the last, time.

San Francisco was a valentine to that city, written by two screenwriters who had grown up there, Anita Loos and Robert Hopkins, and they based the main character Blackie Norton on Wilson Mizner, who was living in Hollywood at the time, but had once run a gambling house on the Barbary Coast. It was a natural part for Clark Gable.

MacDonald played Mary Blake, a singer with operatic aspirations, who is an entertainer at Blackie Norton's saloon, the Paradise. She meets Blackie's rival, John Burley (Jack Holt), who promises to get her a job at the opera, but Blackie refuses to release her from her contract. She is aided by Father Mullin (Spencer Tracy), Blackie's best friend, who runs a mission on the Barbary Coast. He thinks her voice is better suited to the opera and inspirational music. Blackie is furious and spurns her even when she tries to warn him about John Burley's machinations. Of course, they are reunited after suffering through the earthquake. The film actually ends with a shot of the three stars leading the population of the city in 'The Battle Hymn of the Republic.'

The earthquake sequence is a marvel, masterminded by Arnold Gillespie, whose special effects last for a full ten minutes and run from personal encounters with falling chandeliers to a remarkable tile-shedding dome, and were well emphasized by Douglas Shearer's sound department.

The director Woody Van Dyke had trouble with one piece of action, when Blackie, in a rage, hits Father Mullin. After a confrontation with the censors, he spoke to a local priest, who frequently acted as a consultant, and it was he who gave Van Dyke the idea to make the priest turn the other cheek. The film was an instant success. The reviews were enthusiastic and the public soon made it the most profitable M-G-M film of 1936.

Three months after *San Francisco* was released, Irving Thalberg died of pneumonia at the age of 37. The tragedy rocked M-G-M and all of Hollywood.

At the time of his death, Thalberg had two pictures in the last stages of production. The first of these was *Camille* (1936), an adaptation of the novel by Alexandre Dumas *fils*, starring Greta Garbo. The role of the courtesan, Marguerite Gautier, a woman torn between two loves and doomed by her choice, seemed perfect for Garbo, and the film is considered her finest. She was ably supported by a young actor, Robert Taylor, who gives the right air of impetuous ardor to the role of Armand. The difference in their ages gave Garbo

the air of experience that her role demanded, and Taylor looked young enough to have to be protected from youthful folly.

It was a magnificent production. Bernie Hyman, who had taken over for Thalberg, had been give *carte blanche* on this film, and the costumes and sets were as lavish as Adrian and Cedric Gibbons could make them. The cameraman, once again, was William Daniels, who had never made Garbo look more beautiful as when she first meets Armand, or more fragile than in the final scene when she dies in his arms.

The other picture Thalberg left behind had been in production for over two years when he died. This was *The Good Earth* (1936), a story of a Chinese peasant couple based on the novel by Pearl S Buck. The original director, George Hill, had gone to China to shoot backgrounds and collect costumes and props. He even brought back a pair of Chinese water buffalo for the Chinese farm and village being built on the back lot. Just before filming was scheduled to begin, Hill committed suicide, and the direction was taken over by Victor Fleming. Fleming, in turn, became ill and was replaced by Sidney Franklin.

To play the Chinese peasants, Wang and O-Lan, Thalberg cast Paul Muni, who was becoming famous for his biographical pictures at Warner Bros., and Luise Rainer, who had scored a personal triumph with the small part of Anna Held in *The Great Ziegfeld*. The part of the second wife, Lotus, was given to Tilly Losch, another European import, but her accent was still so strong that her voice had to be dubbed. The rest of the cast included such Oriental standbys as Keye Luke, Philip Ahn, Sammee Tong and Richard Loo.

Above: *Eleanor Powell (left) starred as the princess in love with a football player (Nelson Eddy, in photograph) in* Rosalie *(1937). Here she is with Ilona Massey.*
Opposite: *Judy Garland sang 'Everybody Sing' in* Broadway Melody of 1938 *(1937).*

Left: *Luise Rainer and Paul Muni harvest grain as the Chinese peasant couple in* The Good Earth *(1936).*

The highlight of *The Good Earth* is the famous attack of the locusts. Once again Arnold Gillespie's department of special effects came to the fore, although their work was intercut with actual shots of grasshopper swarms in the Middle West.

The Good Earth is not a perfect movie, by any means. It is long, and drags, but it has tremendous sweep. Even the Chinese writer Lin Yutang, who saw it just before its completion at the studio's invitation, could not believe that it wasn't filmed in China. It was deemed a fitting epitaph to Thalberg's career, and when the film was released it carried a foreword – 'To the memory of Irving Grant Thalberg, we dedicate this picture – his last great achievement.'

Hollywood was still borrowing from Broadway, and one of the biggest musical productions that made the journey was *Rosalie* (1937). The plot, which had not been strong to begin with, became sillier as it involved a Ruritanian princess attending college in the United States who falls in love with the captain of the football team. He manages to put down a rebellion in her kingdom, and is rewarded with her hand in marriage. The frailty of the plot was cancelled out by the performers. Eleanor Powell starred as the princess, Nelson Eddy played the football hero. Others on the cast included

Frank Morgan, Ray Bolger and Edna May Oliver.

What really made *Rosalie* different from the usual operetta/musical was its music. The Broadway show had featured a score by George Gershwin and Sigmund Romberg, but that was discarded by M-G-M in favor of one by Cole Porter, which included 'Spring Is in the Air' and 'In the Still of the Night,' as well as a number of classical selections by such odd teammates as Sousa, Tchaikovsky and Reginald DeKoven. The title song became one of the biggest musical numbers ever staged, featuring over 2000 people on a 60-acre set.

A film on smaller scale was *Broadway Melody of 1938* (1937), which also starred Eleanor Powell. The plot, which involved using money won on a steeplechase at Saratoga to back a Broadway play, is forgettable, but the film introduced Judy Garland and featured her in two numbers. The first was 'You Made Me Love You,' prefaced by a little recitative called 'Dear Mr Gable' which she sang looking at his picture. And the second was a big belting number, 'Everybody Sing.' She also had the opportunity to dance with Buddy Ebsen. Mayer was delighted with his new child star, and vowed to make her a bigger hit than Deanna Durbin, who had just left M-G-M for Universal.

Left: *Dame May Whitty, Rosalind Russell and Robert Montgomery starred in* Night Must Fall *(1937).*
Opposite top: *The ghostly Kerbys (Cary Grant and Constance Bennett) watch over Topper (Roland Young) in* Topper *(1937).*

Below: *Captains Courageous (1937) starred Spencer Tracy as the gentle fisherman Manuel, and Freddie Bartholomew as the spoiled kid, Harvey Cheney.*
Opposite below: *Robert Taylor as* A Yank At Oxford *(1937) with Vivien Leigh.*

It was not all sweetness and light at M-G-M. After years of playing leading men and playboys, Robert Montgomery found a part he could sink his teeth into, the charming, but psychotic axe-murderer in *Night Must Fall* (1937). Montgomery had seen the play in New York, and eventually Mayer agreed to let him do it, privately thinking it would teach his recalcitrant star a lesson. Mayer was wrong. With the aid of Dame May Whitty, who had played the role of the menaced old lady on Broadway, Montgomery had a triumph. The film proved very popular, and the star was nominated for the Best Actor Academy Award.

In 1964, M-G-M released a remake starring Albert Finney and Mona Washbourne, with Susan Hampshire in the part of the girl fascinated by the murderer, which had been played by Rosalind Russell in the original. Though it compared with the 1937 version unfavorably, the story still proved popular at the box office.

The actor who beat Robert Montgomery for the Oscar that year was Spencer Tracy, who won for his performance as the Portuguese fisherman Manuel in *Captains Courageous* (1937). Based on the novel by Rudyard Kipling, *Captains Courageous* is the story of a spoiled rich boy, Harvey Cheney, who falls overboard from a liner and is rescued by a schooner going out to join the fishing fleet off the Grand Banks of Newfoundland. Harvey is brought along against his will and forced to work for his keep. He is taken under the wing of Manuel, a Portuguese fisherman aboard the *We're Here*, and eventually learns to carry his weight and makes friends with other members of the crew. When Manuel is swept overboard and killed during the race back to harbor, Harvey has grown enough to be able to bear even that loss and on return to Gloucester, is able to make friends with his father.

The director, Victor Fleming, did an outstanding job bringing the story of Harvey and Manuel to the screen. Where

some directors might have cleaned up the setting, Fleming did not. His schooner looks like a fishing boat, and the crew, though it is made up of Hollywood stalwarts like Lionel Barrymore, as the Captain, and John Carradine, look like any fishing crew.

Freddie Bartholomew gives a brilliant performance as Harvey, which compares with Mickey Rooney's as the captain's son, who has been bred to fishing and looks down on this effete kid who knows nothing about it. It was one of the best adaptations of a novel that Hollywood has achieved.

M-G-M at this time also made a move East, to England, where the first of the M-G-M British-made films, *A Yank At Oxford* (1937) was being filmed at the Denham studios. Starring Robert Taylor, it was the story of a cocky American who gets a scholarship to Oxford and eventually manages to get on the crew for the Oxford-Cambridge boat race. The director was an American, Jack Conway, but most of the actors except Taylor, Barrymore and Maureen O'Sullivan (and she was born in Ireland), were English. One of them was Vivien Leigh, who played a party girl at Oxford.

Back in Hollywood, Hal Roach, whose shorts and serials had long been popular, released a feature through M-G-M. This was *Topper* (1937), based on the novel *The Jovial Ghosts* by Thorne Smith. Transformed for the movies, it told of a young madcap couple who are killed in an automobile accident, but must perform a good deed before they are allowed to leave earth. What they perceive as their good deed is making the hen-pecked life of their banker more fun, or at least bearable.

Cary Grant and Constance Bennett starred as the ghosts George and Marion Kerby, and the timid banker Cosmo Topper was beautifully played by Roland Young. The fun was increased by Roy Seawright's trick photography which allowed the ghosts to vanish and appear at will, including one scene where Miss Bennett is showering (and invisible), but

the water is seen to bounce off her body. Another standout performance was Billie Burke's as the banker's impossible dotty wife. The film was a rare delight and was followed by several sequels and eventually turned into a successful television series.

Late in 1937, M-G-M produced an adaptation of a modest play called *Skidding*, about a Judge Hardy and his family. Renamed *A Family Affair*, it starred Lionel Barrymore as the Judge, Spring Byington as his wife and Mickey Rooney as their son Andy. The following year, came another, *You're Only Young Once*, with Rooney plus Lewis Stone and Fay Holden as the parents. By the third film in the series, *Judge Hardy's Children*, the regulars also included Cecelia Parker as the Hardy's daughter and Ann Rutherford as Andy's girl friend Polly. The series was filmed on the back lot in a typical American small town, built out of remnants of the *David Copperfield* set.

These low-budget pictures were cleaning up at the box office, and Meyer decided to use them to showcase new or promising talent. The fourth film, *Love Finds Andy Hardy* (1938), featured two new players, Judy Garland, as the girl-next-door, Betsy Booth, and Lana Turner as Cynthia, the girl friend of Andy's buddy Jimmy.

The plot concerned Andy's desire for a car. He only needs eight dollars more, and his friend Jimmy, who is going out of town, will pay Andy that if he will keep Cynthia from dating other guys. He does, but that makes Polly jealous, and she won't go to the Christmas dance with him. Jimmy can't pay the eight dollars and Andy thinks he is stuck until the Judge volunteers to pay.

The series was a favorite of Louis B Mayer's, who worked over every detail, complaining at one time when the plot called for a love-lorn Andy to pick at his food. Mayer was incensed. 'No American boy leaves his mother's cooking uneaten.' Heartsick or not, even Andy Hardy ate his vegetables when Mayer spoke.

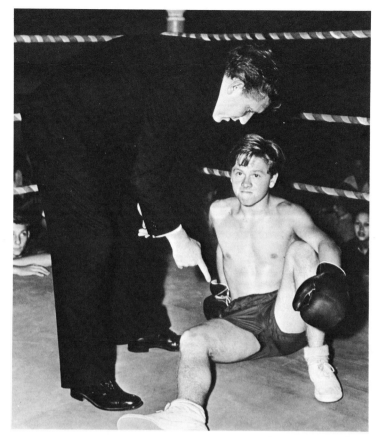

Below: *Mickey Rooney finds Lana Turner, Judy Garland and Ann Rutherford in* Love Finds Andy Hardy *(1938).*

Right: *Spencer Tracy as Father Flanagan encourages Mickey Rooney as Whitey Marsh in* Boys Town *(1938).*

Soon after, Rooney found himself playing a different part, the bad kid Whitey Marsh in *Boys Town* (1938). This was based on the actual attempt by Father Edward Flanagan to provide a home in Nebraska for orphaned boys. Spencer Tracy played Father Flanagan, and his sensitive and sincere performance earned him a second Oscar, which he gave to the real Father Flanagan.

The plot of the movie centered around Flanagan's difficulty in starting the community and especially in getting Whitey Marsh to stay there and accept the restrictions and responsibilities of Boys Town. Though some reviewers found that the fictional drama lessened the impact of Father Flanagan's struggle and ultimate success, the movie-going public didn't care. *Boys Town* became one of M-G-M's most profitable features.

The success of the Andy Hardy series made Mayer look for others. Remembering *Men In White* (1934), a hospital drama, Willis Goldbeck and Harry Ruskin worked up a plot, based on a Max Brand short story, and called it *Young Doctor Kildare* (1938). The lead was played by Lew Ayres, who was most famous for his performance as Paul in *All Quiet On The Western Front* (Universal, 1930). The part of the older, wiser Dr Gillespie was given to Lionel Barrymore, whose chronic arthritis had confined him to a wheelchair.

Ayres made nine films in the series, finishing with *Dr Kildare's Victory* (1941). He spent the war as a conscientious objector. Barrymore stuck it out for five more, with two new assistants, Keye Luke and Van Johnson, before turning in his stethoscope.

While life in Andy Hardy's Carvel and the hospital went on, out in the big world, there was a problem. All the movie companies depended on overseas revenues, and were finding it difficult to maintain the German releases in light of the change in German politics. Thus M-G-M was thought to be taking a risk in producing *Three Comrades* (1938), based on the novel by Erich Maria Remarque about the life of three army friends in Germany in the twenties. Since the screenplay by F Scott Fitzgerald and Edward Paramore emphasized the marriage of one of the three (Robert Taylor) to the tubercular Margaret Sullavan, M-G-M was not truly worried. However, the death of another of the friends in a political riot was cited by a member of the German consular staff as being anti-Nazi. The producer Joseph Mankiewicz refused to change it and the film was released as originally planned.

Besides Taylor and Sullavan, the picture also starred Robert Young and Franchot Tone, as the other ex-army friends. Sullavan, as usual, gave a standout performance as

Above: *Lionel Barrymore played Dr Gillespie, and Lew Ayres was* Young Dr Kildare *(1938), the first of the series.*

Left: Three Comrades *(1938) starred Robert Taylor, Margaret Sullavan, Franchot Tone and Robert Young.*

the tubercular young wife who hastens her own end because it will ease the burden on her husband.

A major production released in 1938 was *Marie Antoinette*, starring Norma Shearer, but this was another movie whose pre-production work had begun under Thalberg. It had also driven Marion Davies from the M-G-M lot. As with *The Barretts of Wimpole Street*, William Randolph Hearst had chosen the story of the doomed French queen as a suitable vehicle for Miss Davies. Once again, Mayer felt that it was not suitable for her talents, but told Hearst she could have it if he would finance the picture. Hearst took that as an insult to Miss Davies, and severed the connection of M-G-M and Cosmopolitan Pictures.

Meyer had won, but was left with a film in its early stages at the time of Thalberg's death. Norma Shearer had been cast in the title role, but didn't feel able to cope with it immediately.

Sidney Franklin had been Thalberg's choice for director, but eventually that job went to W S Van Dyke. As a whole, *Marie Antoinette* is a curiosity. It is certainly not the movie it would have been with Thalberg as producer. It does contain a brilliant performance by Robert Morley as Louis XVI and the production itself is very lush. Shearer's own performance is somewhat overblown, and Tyrone Power, on loan from Twentieth-Century-Fox to play the romantic interest Count Fersen, was overshadowed by the rest of the cast, which included John Barrymore in his last M-G-M appearance, as Louis XV.

The success of *A Yank At Oxford* led to a second movie shot at Denham under similar circumstances. The American director was King Vidor, the American star was Rosalind Russell, but for the lead in the adaptation of A J Cronin's *The Citadel* (1938), M-G-M chose Robert Donat. Donat played the idealistic young doctor whose career takes him from a Welsh mining village to London's Harley Street. His able support came from Ralph Richardson, Rex Harrison and Emlyn

Williams, all of whom were appearing in plays in the West End at the same time they were working on the film.

Clark Gable and Spencer Tracy were costarred again in *Test Pilot* (1938), a thrilling, if frightening view of the test pilot's world. Gable played pilot Jim Lane, who makes a forced landing in Kansas, and meets Ann Barton (Myrna Loy) and her father (Arthur Aylesworth). He takes her with him to complete the flight and they are married. Jim's engineer, Gunner Sloane (Spencer Tracy), tries to make him slow down his pace, but is killed in another test flight.

The three stars managed to rise above what might have been just another melodrama, with the help of a strong screenplay by Vincent Lawrence and Waldemar Young, which emphasizes the toll such adventures take on men's minds and nerves. But the glory of the film was the flying scenes ably directed by Victor Fleming. One reviewer described it as 'a terrifying affair.' that 'it does no good to remember that many of the scenes in the sky were managed in miniature ... or that the persons in whose lives we become interested of course never go off the ground; or that in filming of the tale nobody actually died.' In the same way, that people went to horror movies to scare themselves, they went to see *Test Pilot*, and it received a nomination for Best Picture of 1938.

Later that year, Gable starred in *Idiot's Delight* with Norma Shearer. Based on the antiwar-play by Robert E Sherwood, *Idiot's Delight* told the story of Harry Van, a song-and-dance man, who meets Irene, a mysterious woman, in a hotel on the Swiss border, where they are detained by rumors of war. She is the mistress of an arms dealer, but he is sure that she is the girl he once spent the night with in Lincoln, Nebraska. As bombs begin to fall, she blames her lover and turns back to Harry.

It was a curious choice for M-G-M and both stars. Sherwood wrote the screenplay, adapting his own work, and

Above: *Ralph Richardson (left) and Robert Donat starred in* The Citadel *(1938).*
Right: *Clark Gable, Myrna Loy and Spencer Tracy starred in* Test Pilot *(1938), a film about the intense world of early aviation.*

Opposite: *Tyrone Power as Count Axel de Fersen bids farewell to Norma Shearer as the doomed French queen in* Marie Antoinette *(1938).*

adding a prologue describing the first meeting of two characters. The film also gave theater-goers an opportunity to see Clark Gable dance 'Puttin' On The Ritz' in a delightfully inexpert fashion. All the reviewers thought it first-rate entertainment, but the public wasn't sure.

Norma Shearer was much more at home in *The Women* (1939), an all-star adaptation of Clare Boothe's Broadway hit. The original script had been filled with some fairly racy sexual innuendos but screenwriter Anita Loos managed to change many of them to jokes on female cattiness, and the script was passed by the censors. Besides Shearer as Mary, the betrayed and forgiving wife, the cast included Rosalind Russell as Sylvia, the bitchiest of the women; Joan Crawford as Crystal Allen, the shopgirl who temporarily snares Miss Shearer's husband; Phyllis Povah, repeating her Broadway role as Edith, the perennially pregnant friend and Paulette Goddard as Miriam, the divorcée who marries Miss Russell's husband. To get the required tough performance out of Miss Goddard, director George Cukor asked her to imitate Spencer Tracy.

Clare Boothe said that she had made the character Mary the only one the audience could root for, but the public seemed delighted with the whole cast and followed them from their Park Avenue apartments, dress fittings and exercise classes out to Reno for divorces and back. The scenes between Shearer and Crawford were marvelous, contrasting the nobility of Miss Shearer with the hard-as-nails character of Crawford, giving one of her best performances.

Also due for special commendation were Lucile Watson as Shearer's mother and Virginia Weidler as her daughter. Virginia Weidler was one of the most accomplished of the M-G-M child stars and had made her debut at the age of four in *Surrender* (1931).

Besides the cat fights, *The Women* featured a wonderful fashion parade (shot in Technicolor) and a happy ending. An unusual comedy of love, not a single male was seen in *The Women*, but nobody, least of all the public, seemed to care.

M-G-M tried to repeat their success in 1956 when *The*

Above: *Greer Garson and Robert Donat starred in* Goodbye Mr Chips *(1939).*
Top: The Adventures of Huckleberry Finn *(1939) starred Rex Ingram as Jim, Mickey Rooney as Huck, with Walter Connolly and William Frawley.*

Opposite top: *Harry Van (Clark Gable) and Les Blondes 'Puttin' On The Ritz' in* Idiot's Delight *(1939).*
Opposite far left: *Little Mary (Virginia Weidler) returns a bath sponge to her stepmother, the ex-shop girl Crystal Allan (Joan Crawford) in* The Women *(1939).*
Left: *Count Leon (Melvyn Douglas) finds trying to work his charm on Greta Garbo is uphill work in* Ninotchka *(1939).*

Women was remade as a musical *The Opposite Sex*, with Ann Miller, Joan Blondell, June Allyson and Joan Collins as Crystal Allan. Another change was the addition of men to the cast. The public was not impressed.

After her triumph as *Camille*, Garbo played Polish Countess Marie Waleswska, one of Napoleon's mistresses, in *Conquest* (1937) with Charles Boyer. Then in an imaginative casting triumph, she was signed for *Ninotchka* (1939). The satire of a Soviet envoy in Paris, written by Billy Wilder, Walter Reisch and Charles Brackett, was directed by Ernst Lubitsch, who was responsible for some of the elements that lift this film into the list of Garbo's great ones.

The story concerns three Soviet emissaries who come to Paris to dispose of some of the Russian crown jewels. They are easily and charmingly swayed away from their proletarian cause with the aid of Count Leon (Melvyn Douglas). The Kremlin is not pleased with their reports and send Ninotchka (Garbo) to check on the three emissaries and she too is beguiled by Paris and Count Leon. All ends happily when all four defect from a subsequent mission, and she joins the Count.

Garbo's performance is outstanding as it allows us to imagine her harsh life in the Soviet Union of the thirties. Although jokes are made about the purges, 'there will be fewer but better Russians,' Garbo lets the audience see that it has been life that has marked her, and she becomes a sympathetic character.

The seduction of the three emissaries, Sig Rumann, Felix Bressart and Alexander Granart, is subtly and cleverly implied by voices raised in appreciation of food, wine and women. It is completed by a slow dissolve of their hats on a hatrack, as two cloth caps and a fur hat become two derbies and a silk topper.

Garbo's new image and the film surprised and delighted critics and audiences alike. For her next film, M-G-M cast her as the sedate woman who pretends to be her exotic twin sister in *Two Faced Woman* (1941). It was not a success, and Garbo began an extended leave waiting for a part worthy of her. She is still waiting.

Mickey Rooney's first film of 1939 was *The Adventures of Huckleberry Finn*. It has been said that Mark Twain's novel is impossible to film, although it has been tried several times. Rooney's Huck was described as a teenage abolitionist, which was not Twain's intent. Rex Ingram played Jim, and the film did have good river sequences, but it was not a valid adaptation.

On the eve of war, the M-G-M studio at Denham, in England, was still functioning, and its third production in as many years was *Goodbye Mr Chips* (1939) with Robert Donat and Greer Garson, a new find of Mayer, in the brief but memorable part of Chips' wife. James Hilton's sentimental novel about an English schoolmaster was adapted by R C Sherriff, who had written the play *Journey's End*, Claudine West and Eric Maschwitz, and very ably directed by Sam Wood, who managed to catch the very un-American ambience of an English public school with feeling.

Back at the Culver City studio, M-G-M was involved in something entirely different. *The Wizard of Oz* (1939) had been a successful Broadway hit in 1903, and the book by L Frank Baum was a classic. M-G-M bought the rights, but decided on a new score by Harold Arlen and E Y Harburg. They also wanted Shirley Temple to star, but fortunately a deal with her studio, Twentieth Century-Fox, never materialized, so, by default, the part went to their own Judy Garland.

Garland was 16 at the time, but from the moment she comes on screen nobody cares.

The production was filled with dificulties. The original Tin Woodman, Buddy Ebsen, developed an allergic reaction to his makeup, which involved a powder of pure aluminium, and was replaced by Jack Haley. Margaret Hamilton, as the Wicked Witch of the West, was severely burned when a special effect misfired and melted the green copper-based paint on her hands. She sustained third-degree burns and was out for three months. Her stand-in was also scarred in an accident with a trap door.

After filming, there were other problems. Producer Arthur Freed, who was beginning a career of producing M-G-M musicals, felt that the film was too long, and demanded cuts. So out went 'The Jitterbug,' a popular dance of the period that in no way advanced the plot. Another number cut was 'Over the Rainbow,' but after a preview Freed felt that nothing else could express Dorothy's imaginative yearnings and the song was reinstated. Another cut was the extension of Ray Bolger's dance in 'If I Only Had a Brain.' This was eventually seen as a fragment in the United Artists/M-G-M compilation *That's Dancing* (1985).

The film begins and ends in black-and-white, with a very realistic tornado, and cleverly moves to Technicolor in the land of Oz. The transition is so swift that the door opening into Oz seems to flood the screen with color.

One of the strengths of *The Wizard of Oz* is the charm of Dorothy's three companions, whom the audience first meets as handymen on Uncle Henry and Auntie Em's farm. As one by one they appear in Oz as the Scarecrow (Ray Bolger), the

The Wizard of Oz (1939):
Top left: *Margaret Hamilton as the Wicked Witch of the West.*
Left: *Dorothy (Judy Garland) reaches the gates of the Emerald City, with the Tin Woodman (Jack Haley), the Cowardly Lion (Bert Lahr) and the Scarecrow (Ray Bolger). The doorkeeper is Frank Morgan, who also played the Wizard.*

Opposite top: *Dorothy with Glinda the Good (Billie Burke).*
Opposite below: *Frank Morgan as the Wizard prepares to take Dorothy back to 'the land of E Pluribus Unum' by balloon.*

Above: *Mickey Rooney and Judy Garland 'put on a show' in* Babes in Arms *(1939).*
Opposite: *Mr and Mrs Rhett Butler (Clark Gable and Vivien Leigh) in* Gone With The Wind *(1939).*

Left: *James Stewart and Margaret Sullavan as the feuding co-workers who meet on a blind date in* The Shop Around The Corner *(1939).*

Tin Woodman (Jack Haley) and the Cowardly Lion (Bert Lahr), we know Dorothy is in good hands. In perfect contrast is the utter evil of Margaret Hamilton's Wicked Witch. Director Victor Fleming knew the value of fright, and the scenes with the witch and her horrible flying monkeys are truly scary. Frank Morgan as the Wizard was properly bumbling, removing the thought that magic was responsible for the accomplishments of the four intrepid friends.

The film cost a record $3,200,000 to produce, making it the most expensive M-G-M production up to that time. However, since it has never been out of release, M-G-M is thought to have made a good return on its investment.

After *The Wizard of Oz*, Judy Garland joined her old costar, Mickey Rooney, in *Babes in Arms* (1939), the first of the 'Come on kids, let's put on a show' films. The director was Busby Berkeley, who was much more straightforward with his young cast, including an infant orchestra, and made their theatricals almost believable, at least to start with. The score included only three songs from the original Rodgers and Hart score, 'The Lady Is A Tramp,' the beautiful ballad 'Where Or When' and the title song, but producer Arthur Freed added two of his own songs, 'You Are My Lucky Star,' and 'Good Morning,' as well as 'I Cried For You' and 'God's Country.'

The picture grossed over two million dollars in its first year, and M-G-M found itself with a new cycle of hits, which could be counted on for revenue, allowing the studio to take chances on other films.

One of those films which proved to be surprisingly popular at the box office was *The Shop Around The Corner* (1939) starring Margaret Sullavan and James Stewart. Set in Budapest, the original play by Nikolaus Laszlo was adapted by Samuel Raphaelson and concerned two employees in a novelty shop who loathe one another, but are matched up by a lonely hearts bureau. Once again, Miss Sullavan gave a standout performance, and Stewart was just right as her bumbling nemesis. Frank Morgan, fresh from *The Wizard*, played the shop owner. Others in the cast were Joseph Schildkraut, Felix Bressart and Sara Haden.

The best known M-G-M release of 1939 was not an M-G-M picture at all. Louis B Mayer had been offered the rights to an unpublished novel in 1936, but turned it down because the subject had never been popular at the box office. After some consideration, David O Selznick, who was producing independently at that time, bought the property for $50,000. The story was called *Gone With The Wind* (1939).

After publication, the book became a bestseller and popular interest in Selznick's film was instantaneous. Casting the characters became a popular parlor game. Out of this came one very salient fact, the public would only accept Clark Gable as Rhett Butler. Gable at that time was under exclusive contract to M-G-M, so after consideration, while names like Errol Flynn, Warner Baxter, Basil Rathbone and Ronald Colman were mentioned, Selznick came to an understanding with his father-in-law. M-G-M would lend Gable and provide half the financing (estimated at about $2,500,000) in exchange for world distribution and half the profits.

Having secured Gable's services, Selznick had to convince his star to play the part. As with other roles that he had made his own like Fletcher Christian, Gable didn't want any part of it, but he needed the money for a divorce settlement and so signed a contract.

The part of Scarlett was less easy to cast. There was no popular groundswell centering on one actress. Selznick used

some of the time he needed to let his current distribution deal with United Artists run out in a nationwide talent search for Scarlett O'Hara. Back in Hollywood, most of the leading ladies were also in competition for the part. Screen tests were made of all the most obvious, some of which still exist, so it is possible to see how such diverse actresses as Jean Arthur, Tallulah Bankhead, Joan Bennet, Lana Turner and Margaret Sullavan might have played the role.

By the time Gable was free of his previous commitments and the first of the extensive set was ready, Selznick still had no Scarlett. After some difficulties, the roles of Melanie and Ashley had been given to Olivia de Havilland and Leslie Howard (who was Selznick's first choice, but felt himself to be much too old for the part).

Gone With The Wind *(1939):*
Above: *Rhett (Clark Gable) and Scarlett (Vivien Leigh) escape from the burning city of Atlanta.*
Right: *Scarlett, bored by their talk of war, runs away from the Tarleton twins (Fred Crane and George Reeves) standing on the front steps of Tara.*

Opposite top: *Scarlett searches through the Confederate wounded at the Atlanta station for Dr Meade.*
Below: *Scarlett comes down the staircase of her gaudy mansion in Atlanta looking for Rhett.*

Selznick decided to begin shooting with the burning of Atlanta, using the destruction of the set of some earlier Selznick films, *The Garden of Allah* (1936) and *Little Lord Fauntleroy* (1936) for the city in flames.

It was when the fire began to wane that Selznick's brother Myron introduced him to the young actress accompanying him. It was Vivien Leigh. Selznick had found his Scarlett.

Even with that particular problem solved, filming did not progress smoothly. After three years of work on reducing an novel of 1034 pages to a shooting script, filming began with the opening scene of the book, Scarlett on the front porch of Tara with the Tarleton twins. At that point the director was George Cukor, but two-and-a-half weeks later he was fired. Both female stars were distraught at his dismissal, and continued to consult with him about their characters throughout filming. (Cukor was put on to *The Women*, whose scheduled director Ernst Lubitsch moved over to direct Garbo in *Ninotchka*.)

His replacement was Victor Fleming, who then worked with Selznick on a reworking of the script, eventually returning to the original adaptation by Sidney Howard. Fleming, a great friend of Gable's, resumed shooting two weeks later. When Fleming had a nervous breakdown, he was replaced by Sam Wood. Other shots were directed by Willian Cameron Menzies, the production designer, and Reeves Eason, the second unit director, who had once staged the chariot race in *Ben Hur*.

Filming ended as it had begun, with a retake of the front porch scene, since Selznick had called for Scarlett to wear a different costume than the dress she eventually wears to the barbecue at Twelve Oaks.

The finished film, after cutting, ran for four hours and 45 minutes, and then lost another 65 minutes to achieve its final length of three hours and 40 minutes. Two previews told Selznick he had a success, which the grand opening in Atlanta in December did nothing to contradict. The Academy Awards were equally generous. The picture won a record ten Oscars, including best picture, best actress (Vivien Leigh) best supporting actress (Hattie MacDaniel, as Mammy, the first black performer so honored), best director (Fleming) and six technical or writing awards. The Irving Thalberg Memorial Award 'for the most consistent high level of production achievements by an individual producer' was won by Selznick himself.

After the second release, M-G-M obtained the remaining theatrical rights to the film from one of Selznick's partners. Selznick himself sold his remaining shares when he liquidated his company in 1949.

After many re-releases, attempts to reprint it in Cinemascope, television viewing interrupted by commercials, it is still *Gone With The Wind*, a magnificent example of what Hollywood once could achieve, taking advantage of a system that is now as much of the past as the Confederacy it romanticized so lovingly.

Gone With The Wind (1939):
Right: *Rhett offers his sympathies to the newly widowed Mrs Kennedy and ends up proposing to her.*

Opposite: *Melanie (Olivia de Havilland) and Scarlett meet Ashley Wilkes (Leslie Howard), home on leave for Christmas.*
Below: *Scarlett is distressed to find her waistline has thickened after the birth of her daughter. Mammy (Hattie McDaniel) doesn't approve.*

MGM
GOES TO
WAR

ALTHOUGH WORLD WAR II did not officially begin for the United States until 8 December 1941, the M-G-M studios were instantly affected by the German invasion of Poland. The very profitable overseas market was cut off, though Britain in the first years of the war had a boom in movie attendance.

Closer to home, certain English actors, most notably Leslie Howard, returned to their own country. Howard made a few films in Great Britain and was shot down by German planes in a flight from Lisbon in 1943.

An isolationist United States, however, didn't want any hints of a possible war to come, and it was in this spirit that M-G-M released the last and possible the best of the films called *Broadway Melody. Broadway Melody of 1940* (1940) was another Eleanor Powell vehicle, but her partner this time around was a dancer, Fred Astaire. The never-heavy plot was even lighter, but the public had the pleasure of watching the two masters glide through 'Begin The Beguine' by Cole Porter. Porter was responsible for the rest of the score which also included 'I Concentrate On You.' Others in the cast included George Murphy and Frank Morgan.

M-G-M also borrowed the biopic idea from Warner Bros., who had made it a speciality, and brought out, back to back, *Young Tom Edison* (1940) and *Edison the Man* (1940). The first, starring Mickey Rooney, was somewhat rudely criticized as 'Andy Hardy invents the light bulb,' but under Norman Taurog's direction the fictionalized biography proved to be a charming view of small town America at the end of the nineteenth century. Even better was *Edison the Man* with Spencer Tracy as the inventor. Director Clarence Brown traced Edison's later career, including the invention of the talking machine and the motion picture. This episode contained wonderful scenes duplicating the beginnings of the movies at Edison's workshop/studio in New Jersey.

Above: *Spencer Tracy as the inventor in* Edison the Man *(1940).*
Left: *In* Young Tom Edison *(1940), Mickey Rooney, here with Virginia Weidler, played the inventor as a boy.*

Previous spread: Broadway Melody of 1940 *(1940) starred Eleanor Powell and Fred Astaire.*
Opposite: *Powell and Astaire danced through a Cole Porter score including 'I Concentrate On You' in* Broadway Melody of 1940 *(1940).*

Left: *Langdon Towne (Robert Young) cuts bark for sketching maps for Major Rogers (Spencer Tracy) in* Northwest Passage *(1940).*
Opposite: *Tracy Lord (Katharine Hepburn) is not pleased to find her ex-husband (Cary Grant) opening her wedding presents, while her mother (Mary Nash) and younger sister (Virginia Weidler) look on.*

Below: *Laurence Olivier (second from left) as Mr Darcy and Greer Garson (right) as Elizabeth Bennett change partners (Frieda Inescort, Edward Ashley) in* Pride and Prejudice *(1940).*

Still pursuing the adaptations of great classic novels, M-G-M released *Pride and Prejudice* (1940) starring Laurence Olivier and Greer Garson. Set in the 1830s, rather than Jane Austen's own time, the 1790s, the lush production maintained the correct sense of irony and humor necessary in a comedy of manners, thanks in part to the sensible and witty adaptation by Aldous Huxley and Jane Murfin of Helen Jerome's dramatization of Jane Austen's novel. They even retained some of the most memorable of the novel's lines.

Greer Garson's intelligent and impetuous Elizabeth was the perfect foil for Laurence Olivier's haughty and handsome Mr Darcy. Other in the cast included Edna May Oliver as a formidable Lady Catherine de Bourgh and Mary Boland and Edmund Gwenn as Mr and Mrs Bennett. Though there was some simplification of character, the direction of Robert Z Leonard brought out the plot in all its ramifications and created a very satisfying film.

Another novel to hit the screen in 1940 was Kenneth Roberts' *Northwest Passage*, shot entirely in Technicolor. It had been planned as another huge blockbuster, but ran afoul of its own script. Screen writers Laurence Stallings and Talbot Jennings couldn't condense the second half of the novel, which concerned the actual search for a northwest passage to the Pacific Ocean. Producer Hunt Stromberg decided to use only the first half, and added 'Rogers' Rangers – Book I' to the title.

The film starred Spencer Tracy as the enigmatic Major Rogers and centered on an expedition in the French and Indian War by his Ranger company to rescue English captives and destroy the Indian village at St Francis. To get to St Francis involved an incredible forced march through swamps, bog land and mountains in New York and Quebec, though the film was actually shot in Idaho. Also appearing were Robert Young as the artist Langdon Towne and Walter Brennan as Hunk Marriner, the third of the musketeers.

Cutting the second half of the book left the romantic angle up in the air, and the rivalry between Towne and Rogers for the hand of Elizabeth Browne ended with Towne winning her while Rogers and the rest of the Rangers headed west. In the book, Elizabeth Browne, who was played by Ruth Hussey in the film, married Rogers, as she had in reality.

The reviews were uniformly good, many congratulating the screenwriters for limiting themselves to the first half of the book. Spencer Tracy was on record as saying he was never again in such good physical shape, for the film had demanded that the actors actually work on location and the life had been exhausting.

One of the hits of the Broadway season of 1938/39 was *The Philadelphia Story* by Philip Barry, starring Katharine Hepburn. Louis Mayer wanted it for M-G-M, and he wanted Hepburn to play it, although she was at that time considered 'box office poison.' Mayer was willing to gamble on her, but not to the extent of giving her the costars she wanted, Spencer Tracy and Clark Gable. Eventually she settled on Cary Grant to play her former husband C Dexter Haven and Jimmy Stewart as the newspaper reporter Macaulay Connor.

Barry's sophisticated play and the film were part of a series of comedies poking fun at the American rich, filled with quick repartee and assertive women. It was a part made to order for Hepburn and as Tracy Lord, the brittle heiress torn between her ex-husband and her priggish fiance, not to mention the new emotions created by the reporter, she had a field day. When chastised by her father with the famous speech 'You have a good mind, a pretty face, and a disciplined body that does what you tell it. You have everything it takes to make a lovely woman except the one essential – an understanding heart. Without it, you might just as well be made of bronze,' the audience could see the careful facade crack and she instantly became a sympathetic character.

Grant's performance steals the film as he insinuates the newspaperman and his photographer into the Lord household with the idea of stopping the wedding of his ex-wife. Stewart was 'near perfection,' to quote *The New Republic*, as the poet whose job keeps his feet on the ground, and it was Stewart who won the Academy Award as best Actor for 1940. The screenplay by Donald Ogden Stewart was also honored.

Vivien Leigh followed her triumph as Scarlett O'Hara with *Waterloo Bridge* (1940). Adapted from Robert E Sherwood's play, it was the story of a ballet dancer who falls in love with an English officer. When he is reported killed, she is forced to turn to prostitution to support herself. She meets him again unexpectedly, and is taken to meet his family. He is unaware of her present life, and is astounded when she runs away. The girl, however, had spoken with the hero's mother, and explaining her reasons and her awareness that her life would betray the man she loves. The hero rushes back to London, but is too late to prevent the dancer from committing suicide.

Taylor and Leigh made a beautiful couple, and the supporting cast including Lucile Watson as his mother, C Aubrey Smith as his great uncle and Maria Ouspenskya as the ballet mistress. The film was taken out of the romantic melodrama class by the sheer beauty of its production. The direction by Mervyn Le Roy cleverly pinpointed certain aspects of the dancer's life in theatrical boarding houses, contrasting them to the assured, if false, aristocratic background of the hero.

A 1956 remake called *Gaby*, starred Leslie Caron and John Kerr, but was less successful than the 1940 version, or even the orignal made by Universal in 1931.

M-G-M scored one of their biggest successes in 1941 with *Ziegfeld Girl*. It was an extravaganza, disguising a plot that wasn't young in *Sally, Irene & Mary* (1925), tracing the lives of three showgirls in the Follies. One, Judy Garland, became a star, the second Hedy Lamarr, married well and the third, Lana Turner, became an alcoholic. Once again Busby Berkeley had a field day with over '100 beautiful girls' in such numbers as 'You Stepped Out Of A Dream,' featuring LaMarr and Turner, and Judy Garland's renditions of 'I'm Always

Below: *Vivien Leigh as a young ballerina meets a young officer (Robert Taylor) on* Waterloo Bridge *(1940).*

Opposite: *Hedy Lamarr was one of the 'Glorified Girls' in* Ziegfeld Girl *(1941), with Lana Turner and Judy Garland.*

Chasing Rainbows' and 'Minnie From Trinidad.' Lana Turner as the third showgirl gave a promising performance, especially when she fell to her death after recalling for only a second, merely by a change in her posture, her success in the Follies.

After *Ziegfeld Girl*, Judy Garland went into *Babes on Broadway* (1941), joining Mickey Rooney, Virginia Weidler, Ray MacDonald and Richard Quine in 'putting on a show.' This time the object of their concern was a settlement house, and the young cast members were supposed to be aspiring actors and actresses. Once again Busby Berkeley directed and the musical numbers included a wonderful 'Hoe Down' and Judy's renditions of 'How About You' and 'Franklin D Roosevelt Jones.' Both Mickey and Judy had sequences in which they imitated legendary performers of the stage, Judy did Sarah Bernhardt and Blanche Ring, while Mickey took on Sir Harry Lauder and George M Cohan.

The Philadelphia Story had marked a turning point in the career of Katharine Hepburn, and she took advantage of its success to ask Mayer for a few favors concerning her next picture, *Woman of the Year* (1941). She had chosen the vehicle by two unknown screenwriters, Ring Lardner Jr and Michael Kanin, and she wanted Spencer Tracy as her costar and George Stevens as director. She got them both.

Woman of the Year (1942) was the story of two newspaper reporters, Sam Craig and Tess Harding, who have been feuding in their columns, but then they meet, fall in love and

marry! Tess is not willing to change her life, and Sam eventually walks out, the night Tess is named Woman of the Year. Sam goes on a bender and Tess, despite her ignorance of the subject, writes his sports column for him. Sam realizes that she does care for him, and they are reunited.

The two stars complemented one another to a degree that astounded many who had predicted fireworks from two people with such opposing temperaments. Tracy's easy style was in perfect harmony with Hepburn's tense brilliance. M-G-M had another winning team and would certainly take advantage of it.

Spencer Tracy's next film, however, was *Dr Jekyll and Mr Hyde* (1941), and his female costars were Ingrid Bergman and Lana Turner. M-G-M was certainly not the first studio to film Robert Louis Stevenson's strange tale. There had been eight previous versions including one made in Denmark, but the most famous was shot in 1931 by Rouben Mamoulian for Universal, starring Fredric March.

Director Victor Fleming based his version rather closely on Mamoulian's, though using a brand-new screenplay by John Lee Mahin. Tracy decided to eschew the usual grotesque makeup as Mr Hyde, and used a strange collection of expressions plus a bit of extra hair on his eyebrows to show his transformation into the good doctor's less attractive alter-ego. It was not a part that favored Tracy.

The real discovery was Ingrid Bergman as the barmaid Ivy, who is rescued by Dr Jekyll and later seduced and murdered

Opposite: *Mickey Rooney and Judy Garland led the young cast of* Babes on Broadway *(1941).*
Right: *Lana Turner and Ingrid Bergman played the fiancée and mistress of Spencer Tracy in* Dr Jekyll and Mr Hyde *(1941).*

Below: *Spencer Tracy and Katharine Hepburn as the newspaper reporters Sam Craig and Tess Harding in* Woman of the Year *(1942).*

by Mr Hyde. Originally Bergman had been slated to play Beatrix, the doctor's fiancée, and Lana Turner had the part of Ivy. Reluctantly, the studio allowed them to switch parts. Miss Bergman at least gave a good performance, but the whole film was castigated as 'a preposterous mixture of hokum and psychological balderdash...' or as 'handsome, stuffy and pompous hokum, with nothing new to say.'

Hokum might have been one of the criticisms leveled at *Mrs Miniver* (1942), for that film gave a most untrue picture of England at war. However, it was great propaganda, and at the time of its release the United States was also at war. The audience was primed to believe and hope that this was the way they would face assault by the enemy.

The performances of the two lead characters, Greer Garson and Walter Pidgeon, certainly lifted *Mrs Miniver* out of the usual movie rut. The audience was simply swept along into the never-never land of M-G-M's England from its flower shows, complete with rivalries between the stationmaster (Henry Travers) and the local landowner (Dame May Whitty), to its Churchillian sermons by the rector in the pulpit of a half-bombed village church. It was perhaps at its best when the Minivers' personal war was forgotten and they joined the

Opposite: *Greer Garson and Walter Pidgeon comfort their children Christopher Severn and Clare Sandars during an air raid in* Mrs Miniver *(1942).*

Above: *Greer Garson bids farewell to Ronald Colman who suffers from amnesia and has forgotten their marriage in* Random Harvest *(1942).*

common war. The little Armada to rescue the stranded army at Dunkirk is powerfully portrayed, as is the occasion that Mrs Miniver catches a downed German flyer in her garden. The scenes in the air-raid shelter are remarkably believable, if only for the clever set decoration that did not ignore details like a delicate bedside clock, and a tin of petit beurre biscuits.

It was probably the subject matter rather than the treatment that actually gave seven Academy Awards to the film, but it was certainly the right movie for the time.

One of the films also nominated for Best Picture that year was *Random Harvest* (1942) adapted from the novel by James Hilton. *Random Harvest* began at the end of World War I, when an amnesiac (Ronald Coleman) escapes from a military hospital, and is taken in by a music-hall performer (Greer Garson, who holds the plot up long enough to do an imitation of Sir Harry Lauder). They are married and several

years later he goes to Liverpool for a job interview when he is struck down by a cab and regains his memory, up to the time of the war, forgetting everything that has happened since – wife, child and country cottage. He returns to his own rather palatial home, and his rather high-powered job. He also encounters the rest of the family, who are, for the most part, parasites. The exception is a young cousin (Susan Peters) with whom he becomes emotionally involved. They are at the point of picking hymns for the wedding, when a melody makes him feel that he must not go through with the ceremony. Breaking their engagement, he throws himself into his work, which is made easier by his new secretary, who turns out to be the wife he has forgotten.

Eventually, just before World War II is declared, she takes him back to the cottage where they were once so happy, and his memory is fully restored.

It was certainly the performances of Ronald Colman and Greer Garson which saved *Random Harvest*, but any weaknesses of the plot were certainly the fault of James Hilton, not the screen writers or the director Mervyn LeRoy, and the film was a tremendous hit.

By 1942, Judy Garland had grown up, even by M-G-M standards, and she received her first star billing in *For Me And My Gal* (1942), which costarred Gene Kelly in his movie debut. Kelly played an opportunistic vaudevillian who takes advantage of Garland's love and talent. The somewhat depressing plot was lifted by the musical numbers which included the title song, 'When You Wore A Tulip,' 'Till We Meet Again' and Judy's poignant 'After You've Gone.' The director was Busby Berkeley, and George Murphy co-starred.

One of the aspects of the war with which the United States had already become familiar was evacuees and war orphans. M-G-M used their plight as the basis for *Journey for Margaret* (1942). Robert Young starred with Laraine Day as an American correspondent and his wife who rescue and adopt two children orphaned by the blitz. The older of the two was played by Angela Maxine O'Brien who had made her movie debut the previous year in *Babes On Broadway* at the age of four. Following the success of *Journey* she changed her first name to Margaret.

Journey for Margaret was the last of W S Van Dyke's features. The veteran M-G-M director had begun as an assistant to D W Griffith, and directed his first picture, *War Paint*, starring Tim McCoy, in 1926. He was 53 at the time of his death in 1942.

The most unusual film of 1942 was certainly *Cabin in the Sky*, the first all-black movie since *The Green Pastures* (1936, Warner Bros.) and the first M-G-M one since King Vidor's *Hallelujah* in 1929.

Based on a successful Broadway show of 1940, *Cabin in the Sky*, a variation on the legend of *Faust*, was the story of the

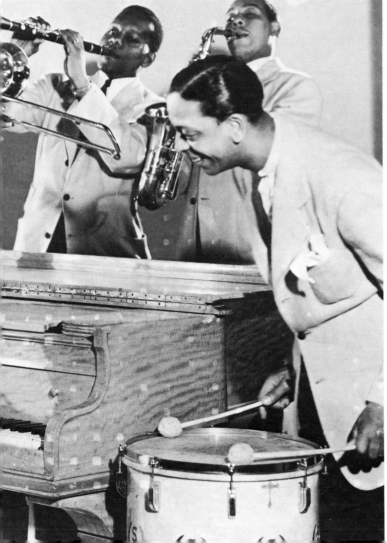

battle for one man's soul between his wife and heaven on one side and the devil and a schemer named Georgia Brown on the other. The soul in contention, Little Joe, was played by Eddie 'Rochester' Anderson and his wife Petunia by Ethel Waters. The forces of heaven were led by Kenneth Spencer as the Lawd's General. Rex Ingram was Lucifer Jr, and Georgia Brown was played by Lena Horne, who sang the seductive 'Honey In The Honeycomb.' Other songs which had been in the Broadway show included 'Taking A Chance On Love,' sung by Ethel Water with Eddie Anderson on guitar, 'Li'l Black Sheep' and 'In My Old Virginia Home.' Added to the film were 'Going Up' by Duke Ellington, 'Things Ain't What They Used To Be' and the best known song from the show, 'Happiness Is Just A Thing Called Joe,' sung by Ethel Waters. *Cabin in the Sky* was the first M-G-M picture directed by Vincente Minnelli, and the rest of the cast included Louis Armstrong, Butterfly McQueen, Ruby Dandridge and Duke Ellington and his Orchestra.

By 1943, the studio had truly geared up for war with the release of pictures like *Assignment in Brittany*, based on the novel by Helen MacInnes, *A Guy Named Joe*, a fantasy about a dead pilot who returns to earth to aid a young fighter, and *Bataan*, considered one of the best battle movies.

Bataan was a re-enactment of a heroic rear-guard suicide mission of a company who volunteered to protect the American retreat. The star was Robert Taylor, who was excellent as the last survivor of the patrol, the hard-bitten sergeant who holds the company together and eventually buries them one by one as they are picked off by the approaching Japanese.

Above: *Robert Walker, Robert Taylor, Kenneth Spencer and Philip Terry bury one of their dwindling squad in* Bataan *(1943).*

Left: *Ann Sothern and Margaret Sullavan played army nurses on Bataan in* Cry Havoc *(1943).*

Opposite top: *Robert Taylor as the American conductor who joins his Russian wife (Susan Peters) in the defense of her motherland in* Song of Russia *(1943).*

Opposite below: *Gene Kelly and Jean-Pierre Aumont were French soldiers escaping from POW camp in* The Cross of Lorraine *(1943).*

Though made entirely on an M-G-M sound stage, the art direction of Cedric Gibbons and the special effects of Arnold Gillespie and Warren Newcombe spared no expense in making the set as realistic as possible.

A companion piece was *Cry Havoc* (1943), an all-female drama about nurses on Bataan, which starred Joan Blondell, Margaret Sullavan and Ann Sothern. As with *Bataan*, the close quarters gave director Richard Thorpe the opportunity to explore the lives of his characters. At exactly the same time *Cry Havoc* was being shot, on an neighboring sound stage Tay Garnett was directing one of the first wartime prisoner-of-war films, *The Cross of Lorraine*. The film starred Jean-Pierre Aumont, Gene Kelly, Peter Lorre and Sir Cedric Hardwicke, in a story of Frenchmen who surrender too easily to the Germans and undergo torture before they escape to join the resistance.

A war film with a different slant was *Song of Russia* (1943), starring Robert Taylor. Taylor was worried about its timely pro-communist sympathies. The story about an American composer and his Russian wife whose marriage is shaken by her commitment to fight alongside her comrades was M-G-M's way of honoring its ally, but audiences weren't convinced. It is best remembered for the glorious score by Herbert Stothart with an assist from Tchaikovsky and other Russian composers.

The last Mickey Rooney-Judy Garland musical was *Girl Crazy* (1943), and the scene shifted to the west. This time Mickey had been sent out to Cody College for chasing girls back east. He falls in love with the dean's granddaughter (Judy Garland) and together they put on a rodeo to save the college from financial collapse. It was not an original plot, since it was based on the Broadway hit by George and Ira Gershwin of 1930, and had been filmed in 1932 by RKO-Radio. For once, most of the original Gershwin score, featuring such stand-bys as 'Embraceable You,' 'Bidin' My Time,' 'Fascinatin' Rhythm' and the lovely ballad 'But Not For Me' was retained. The director was Busby Berkeley and he directed the big finale of 'I Got Rhythm,' which featured Tommy Dorsey and his Orchestra. Norman Taurog replaced Berkeley halfway through the film, but the change is undetectable.

Rooney's next movie was a change of pace as he played Homer Macauley in *The Human Comedy* (1943). Based on the sentimental yet optimistic novel by William Saroyan, *The Human Comedy* was a series of loving vignettes describing the life of a family during the war years. With his older brother Marcus in the service, Homer must be the man of the family to his widowed mother, older sister and younger brother. He takes a job as a telegraph delivery boy, which brings him in contact with many of the residents of Ithaca, California.

Frank Morgan played the old telegraph operator who dies of a heart attack while receiving notices of Marcus' death in action. Others in the cast included Fay Bainter as Mrs Macauley, Donna Reed as sister Bess and Van Johnson as Marcus, seen in scenes in the army with his friend Tobey George (John Craven).

Saroyan won an Oscar for the original story, which was lovingly preserved by Howard Estabrook and director Clarence Brown. The film was a sentimental favorite of Louis B Mayer's but received mixed reviews. However, the small town exhibitors did very well with it.

The small budget unit run by Harry Rapf at M-G-M had a property that involved another star search. This was *Lassie Come Home* (1943), the story of a Scottish collie. There hadn't been a great dog star since Warner Bros.' Rin-Tin-Tin. The producer Sam Marx advertised for a mass interview, which came to nothing, sent a trainer, Rudd Weatherwax, scouring the Hollywood Hills for collies, and eventually settled on the trainer's own pet, a companionable but not championship-caliber collie named Pal.

Lassie is the pet of Roddy McDowall, the son of an impoverished Scottish shepherd, who is forced to sell the dog for money. Lassie eventually is returned to her rightful owner through the kindness of a small girl, who was played by a British evacuee named Elizabeth Taylor. Miss Taylor inherited the role when the child who was originally cast

Opposite top: The Human Comedy *(1943) starred Donna Reed, Mickey Rooney, Dorothy Morris and Fay Bainter.*
Opposite below: *Tommy Dorsey and his Orchestra joined Mickey Rooney and Judy Garland for the finale of* Girl Crazy *(1943).*

Right: *Roddy McDowall and Pal in* Lassie Come Home *(1943). As Lassie, Pal became the first dog star since Rin-Tin-Tin.*

found that the brightness of the lights hurt her eyes. Others in the cast included Donald Crip, Elsa Lanchester and Nigel Bruce. The director was Fred Wilcox.

One of the most popular films of 1944 was *Meet Me In St Louis*, a nostalgic musical set at the time of the 1903 World's Fair and starring Judy Garland. Based on Sally Benson's recollections of her girlhood, *Meet Me In St Louis* was a series of vignettes about the Smith family, whose happy provincial lives are threatened by the possible transfer of their father to New York. Within this framework, the audience shares the usual family trials and tribulations, the engagement of the eldest daughter, the last Hallowe'en and Christmas, the attachment of another daughter to 'The Boy Next Door.' And it is with great relief that the audience learns with the family that the impending transfer is cancelled and the family is to stay in St Louis.

Directed by Vincente Minnelli, the film had a wonderful candy-box freshness and the carefully integrated songs, like 'Have Yourself A Merry Little Christmas,' 'The Trolley Song' and 'Under the Bamboo Tree' duet sung and danced by Judy Garland and Margaret O'Brien added sparkle. Also in the cast were Lucille Bremer as the oldest sister, Mary Astor and Leon Ames as the parents and Tom Drake as the boy next door.

Oddly enough, nobody at the studio had confidence in the

project at its outset, and producer Arthur Freed and Minnelli had to beg for everything, including the story and the funds to rebuild a reproduction of a St Louis street at the beginning of the century. They even had to beg Garland to accept the role of Esther Smith, which was later said to have been her favorite.

Freed and Minnelli were proved correct in their estimation of the film's worth. It found a ready audience in wartime America, and became the second biggest grossing film, up to that time, after *Gone With The Wind*. Even the expensive St Louis set earned back its initial cost of $100,000, for it was rented and used many times after shooting on the film was complete.

It is not every film that gives a new verb to the English language. *Gaslight* (1944) began as a play called *Angel Street*, a melodrama by Patrick Hamilton. It was first filmed in England, as *Gaslight*, in 1940 with Anton Walbrook, Diana Wynyard and Frank Pettingill. In 1944 M-G-M remade it with Ingrid Bergman, Charles Boyer and Joseph Cotten. (In England, the M-G-M version is known as *Murder in Thornton Square*.)

The plot of *Gaslight* concerns a pianist who marries the niece of an opera singer and proceeds to try to make her think she is going mad, with a series of strange incidents. He eventually proves to be the aunt's murderer and had married the girl only for the opportunity to search the house at his leisure for the woman's famous jewels.

The reviews found Miss Bergman magnificent as the near-victim, and she won the Academy Award as Best Actress for her performance. Boyer was wonderfully menacing as the persecuting husband. Academy Awards were also presented to the four men responsible for the lush art direction which beautifully depicted the right air of gentility. The emotional outbreaks were much more startling for taking place in such a refined setting.

George Cukor directed and managed to allow Miss Bergman to move close to hysteria without going over the edge,

and her air of menace when her husband has been captured and begs for his freedom is wonderfully controlled. Making her debut as the maid attracted to her master was Angela Lansbury, who was nominated for Best Supporting Actress.

Another film set in Victorian England was *The Picture of Dorian Gray* (1945), a curious experiment directed by Albert Lewin, who had been associate producer on many of Thalberg's classical adaptations in the thirties, and based on the novel by Oscar Wilde. Hurd Hatfield starred as the beautiful young man who is corrupted by the worldly Lord Henry Wooton (George Sanders), and whose excesses distort the portrait he keeps hidden.

Once again M-G-M production values accentuate the

Opposite: *Margaret O'Brien and Judy Garland sing 'Under The Bamboo Tree' in* Meet Me In St Louis *(1944).*

Right: *Ingrid Bergman looks fearfully at her sadistic husband, Charles Boyer, in* Gaslight *(1944).*

Below: *Angela Lansbury the music hall singer greets Hurd Hatfield in* The Picture of Dorian Gray *(1945).*

elegance of the period, and made Dorian's investigations into the less salubrious parts of London take on a frightening fairy-tale aspect, filled as they are with hunchbacks, cripples, fog and dim lights. As Dorian, Hurd Hatfield's wonderfully subdued performance and his beautiful face, which contrasted brilliantly with the vile portrait painted by Ivan Albright, were sensational.

At the end, he destroys the portrait, and in doing so kills himself and is transformed into the fiend he is, while the portrait returns to its classic perfection. Cleverly, the audience has been appalled by his life, not by what has been seen, but in what has been imagined.

The film uses a curious device of narration and very few closeups of people, depending on images and wonderfully suggestive details. The cast included Angela Lansbury as a music hall singer, and Lowell Gilmore as the portrait painter.

Another Oscar Wilde story was the basis of *The Canterville Ghost* (1944), a comedy about GIs billeted in a haunted castle. The film starred Robert Young as one of the GIs, Charles Laughton as Sir Simon de Canterville, the ghost in question, and Margaret O'Brien as the child who can see the spirit. The direction by Jules Dassin was too heavy-handed for such a light, gentle film, and the performance of the good deed which allows the ghost to rest was not the climax it should have been.

Child-star Elizabeth Taylor made *Jane Eyre* (1944) while she was on a loan-out to Twentieth Century-Fox after *Lassie*

Come Home. Then she was signed for Velvet Brown, the lead in *National Velvet* (1944), an adaptation of Enid Bagnold's novel about a young girl who wins a horse in a lottery, and trains it to run in the Grand National. An accident to the jockey forces her to ride the horse herself, and she is, of course, the winner.

Her costars included Mickey Rooney as Mi Taylor, the jockey, and Donald Crisp and Anne Revere as her parents. Miss Revere won the Academy Award for Best Supporting Actress for her performance as the understanding Mrs Brown.

Clarence Brown's direction and the beautiful photography by Leonard Smith revealed the Brown household in all its detail, as well as the brilliantly paced and shot finale of the race. It was all the more remarkable since the studio re-created the racetrack at Aintree, as well as the rest of its 'England' for the film.

Throughout the war, movie studios continued to make films set on both theaters of the war. One of the most ambitious was *The Seventh Cross* (1944), starring Spencer Tracy. Actually set in a concentration camp before the outbreak of war, *The Seventh Cross* described the escape of seven inmates. The commandant erects a cross for each man and as they are recaptured, they are crucified. The seventh cross is for George Heisler (Tracy), an embittered man who learns to trust others during his escape. Thanks to those that aided him, the seventh cross remains empty.

Above: *In the jockeys' dressing room before the Grand National, Mi Taylor (Mickey Rooney) explains to another jockey (Wally Cassell) that Velvet (Elizabeth Taylor) doesn't speak English in* National Velvet *(1944).*
Right: *Jessica Tandy and Hume Cronym aid Spencer Tracy as the escaping George Heisler in* The Seventh Cross *(1944).*

Opposite: *Sir Simon de Canterville (Charles Laughton) shows Robert Young his place in the family genealogy in* The Canterville Ghost *(1944).*

Hume Cronyn, Jessica Tandy and Signe Hasso costarred and Fred Zinnemann, at the beginning of his long and honorable career, directed. The screenplay by Helen Deutsch used little dialogue, and established its suspense through cutting and gesture. The movie was advertised by letting Spencer Tracy's stand-in make his way as a man on the run from New York to California without being recognized, despite the number of posters advertising the gimmick, and the film.

In an entirely different war movie, Tracy played Lieutenant Colonel James Doolittle in *Thirty Seconds Over Tokyo* (1944), a painstaking reconstruction of the Doolittle bombing raid in 1942. The Dalton Trumbo screenplay also followed the pilots after the raid, as they crashlanded at sea, to be washed up on the coast of China, and eventually make their way back to the unit. Van Johnson and Robert Walker co-starred as fliers in Doolittle's squadron, and Phyllis Thaxter provided the love interest as Johnson's wife. Despite the billing, Tracy had little to do in the film, which centered on Johnson and Walker.

Once more M-G-M invoked the master showman with the release of *Ziegfeld Follies* (1945), a return to the revue format that had been so popular with the birth of sound. There was no plot, but the picture opened with Ziegfeld (William Powell, once again) in heaven planning the ultimate Follies to use the great talent at his disposal. Highlights included three dance scenes by Fred Astaire. The first, 'Limehouse Blues,' he danced with Lucille Bremer in a fantasy, reminiscent of *Broken Blossoms*, which had a prologue and epilogue shot on an English street left over from *Dorian*

Above: *Spencer Tracy as Lieutenant-Colonel Doolittle briefs his officers before the attack in* Thirty Seconds Over Tokyo *(1944).*

Ziegfeld Follies *(1945)*:
Opposite top: *Lucille Bremer and Fred Astaire in 'Limehouse Blues'.*
Right: *Judy Garland holds a 'star's' press conference.*

Gray. The second, 'The Babbitt and The Bromide,' Astaire danced with Gene Kelly. It was the only time the two appeared together in a movie, until they both served as hosts in *That's Entertainment, Part II*. The third number was 'This Heart Of Mine,' and once again his partner was Miss Bremer.

Other performers included Lena Horne singing 'Love,' Esther Williams in an underwater ballet, Judy Garland doing a wonderful takeoff of *the* Hollywood star and a comic sketch by Fannie Brice that was cut for foreign distribution.

Another musical with little plot, but lots of dancing, was also released in 1945. This was *Anchors Aweigh*, with Gene Kelly and Frank Sinatra as two sailors on leave in Hollywood. Kathryn Grayson, who had first played in *Andy Hardy's Private Secretary* (1941), and Pamela Britton were the girls. Kelly also danced 'The Worry Song' with Jerry the Mouse, courtesy of William Hanna and Joseph Barbera, who provided the animation.

Other sensational numbers included 'All Of A Sudden My Heart Sings,' 'What Makes the Sunset?' and 'I Fall In Love Too Easily.'

Judy Garland had two triumphs that year. In *The Clock* (1945), a rare non-singing role, she fell in love and married soldier Robert Walker on a 48-hour leave. The original director was Fred Zinnemann but he was replaced at Judy's request by Vincente Minnelli, whom she subsequently married.

The second film was *The Harvey Girls* (1945), an unusual Western about the establishment of decent restaurants along a southwestern railroad by entrepreneur Fred Harvey. Garland played one of the waitresses who finds herself competing with Em, the dance hall hostess (Angela Lansbury) for the affections of John Hodiak. The western saloons find the incursion of Harvey's restaurants a threat, and the regulars at the Alhambra Bar and Dance Hall steal a load of meat destined for Harvey's. It is Judy and her two six-guns who hold up the saloon and force a return of the meat.

The songs included 'Wait And See,' 'In the Vally When The Evening Sun Goes Down' and 'On the Atchison Topeka and Santa Fe,' which won the Academy Award as the best song of 1945.

By the time *The Harvey Girls* was released, World War II was over. The public was satiated with war movies, and seemed ready to take any escapist fare to their hearts. Musicals, biographies and movies about children or animals all did well at the box office, but a new, cynical kind of movie was also making itself known. The audience had changed in the past six years. They were no longer as innocent or as parochial as they had been. The end of the war meant that the European studios would also resume filming, as indeed some already had, which would bite into the American and British movie monopoly. M-G-M was faced with change, and no idea what the post-war years would bring.

Top right: *Robert Walker and Judy Garland starred in* The Clock *(1945).*
Right: *Angela Lansbury as the dance-hall hostess was Judy Garland's rival in* The Harvey Girls *(1945).*

Opposite: *Frank Sinatra and Gene Kelly played sailors on leave in* Anchors Aweigh *(1945).*

DECLINE
AND
FALL

M-G-M AND THE OTHER studios all believed the end of the war meant a return to the palmy days before the war. The boys, including such M-G-M stars as Clark Gable, Robert Taylor and James Stewart, would come home, and the profitable European market would reopen. They were certainly not expecting changes in movie-going habits and taste which would lead to lower box office revenues, or interference from the New York office of Loew's Inc, which was, of course, still the parent company of M-G-M.

Also in the wings was the Supreme Court ruling on the structure of the motion picture companies who produced, distributed and exhibited their own product, a practice which smacked of monopoly. This cut hard into expected profits for all the movie companies involved. The actual percentage of profits from exhibiting compared to that from rentals was a closed subject.

None of this was seen in the films of 1946, least of all in *The Yearling*, starring Gregory Peck and Jane Wyman, an adaptation of Margery Kinnan Rawlings' novel of a back-woods boy and his pet fawn. The project had begun back in 1941, with a different cast, headed by Spencer Tracy and Anne Revere,

and a different director, Victor Fleming. Fleming was replaced by King Vidor, but by that time the production was behind schedule, the fawn had grown up and Mayer had cancelled the film.

The success of *Lassie Come Home* had given Mayer a new perspective on animal pictures, and production on *The Yearling* was resumed with a new cast, including a young boy named Claude Jarman Jr as Jody, in place of Gene Eckman, under the direction of Clarence Brown. The film, which was shot on location in Florida by Charles Rosher and Leonard Smith, was beautiful to look at, a dream of dark Everglades waterways and scrub forest, with a magnificent bear hunt, but many critics felt that Paul Osborn's screenplay was not faithful to the original and thought Peck and Wyman miscast as the boy's parents. The public didn't seem to care and the picture, its two stars and its director were all nominated for Academy Awards. Young Claude Jarman was honored with a miniature Oscar for the best performance by a child, an award previously given to Shirley Temple, Mickey Rooney, Judy Garland and Margaret O'Brien.

Robert Montgomery, newly returned from the Navy,

Left: *Claude Jarman Jr played Jody in* The Yearling *(1946).*
Previous spread: *Audie Murphy (left) and Bill Mauldin in* The Red Badge of Courage *(1951).*

Opposite top: *Robert Montgomery as Philip Marlowe, with Audrey Totter in* Lady In The Lake *(1946).*
Opposite bottom: *Lana Turner and John Garfield were the scheming lovers in* The Postman Always Rings Twice *(1946).*

starred in and directed an unusual adaptation of Raymond Chandler's *Lady In The Lake* (1946). Screenwriter Steve Fisher retained the first person narrative of the Philip Marlowe thriller and the movie was filmed from Marlowe's point of view, literally, with the camera being held at eye level. The audience only saw the star when he was reflected in a mirror. The novel camera angle also slowed down the pace of the hard-boiled private eye investigation. This unpopular experiment was Montgomery's last film for M-G-M, ending an association that went back to *So This Is College* (1929).

Another unusual film, whose reception should have given M-G-M a hint of the change in the public's taste, was *The Postman Always Rings Twice* (1946). Based on the novel by James M Cain, the plot centered around the fatal attraction of a married woman and her lover who scheme to kill the woman's husband. The direction by Tay Garnett was skillful and hard-bitten, just like the novel, fortunately, since the screenplay by Harry Ruskin and Niven Busch slightly sentimentalized its hard edge. Lana Turner, always dressed in white as the wife, gave the performance of her career and John Garfield was vulnerable, yet tough, as the drifter who is caught in her plot, from the moment he sees her legs and then the rest of her as he retrieves her dropped lipstick. Cecil Kellaway played her aging husband, the owner of the slightly seedy roadside restaurant where the action takes place.

The novel had been filmed twice before, in 1939 as *Le Dernier Tournant* by Pierre Chenal, and in 1942 by Italy's Luchino Visconti as *Ossessione*. A remake with Jack Nicholson and Jessica Lange was released in 1981.

Minnelli. The rest of the cast were under the direction of Richard Whorf.

Another returned soldier was Mickey Rooney, who appeared in *Love Laughs At Andy Hardy* (1946), the 15th in the Andy Hardy series.

At 26, Rooney was a little long in the tooth to be convincing as an adolescent and the film was not a success. In 1958, the studio tried to revive the series again with *Andy Hardy Comes Home*, and reunited the original members of the family, except for Lewis Stone, who had died. It was not a hit either, most likely because of the change in moviegoers' taste. People were no longer interested in the small crises that had made the series so successful, and those that remembered the Hardy family in their prime were not ready for Andy to assume the role as *paterfamilias*.

Arthur Freed, who headed the important M-G-M musical unit, had an unexpected success with the remake of *Good News* (1947). Peter Lawford and June Allyson starred in what has been called 'the quintessential college musical.' The plot involved the suspension of the star football player for bad grades, and his developing romantic attachment to the tutor who finally helps him to pass his exams.

The script, adapted from a 1927 Broadway hit, might have been slight, but the music by Buddy de Sylva, Lew Brown and Ray Henderson featured such wonderful songs as 'The Best Things in Life are Free,' 'Lucky in Love,' and the unforgettable

Another box-office triumph was *Till The Clouds Roll By* (1946), a biography of composer Jerome Kern, with Robert Walker in the lead. The predictable plot was aided immeasurably by the musical numbers which included Lena Horne singing 'Can't Help Lovin' That Man Of Mine' and 'Why Was I Born.' Other Kern songs that were showcased were 'The Last Time I Saw Paris' sung by Dinah Shore, 'Ol' Man River' sung by Frank Sinatra, and the great ballad 'All the Things You Are' sung by Tony Martin. Judy Garland appeared to sing 'Who,' 'Look For The Silver Lining' and 'Sunny,' in sequences specially directed by her husband Vincente

Right: *June Allyson and Peter Lawford lead the chorus in 'The Varsity Drag' from* Good News *(1947).*
Below right: *The Patourel sisters, Marguerite and Marianne (Donna Reed and Lana Turner) meet William Ozanne (Richard Hart) in* Green Dolphin Street *(1947).*

Opposite: *Frank Sinatra was one of the many stars in the musical biography of Jerome Kern,* Till The Clouds Roll By *(1946).*
Below: *Mickey Rooney was still playing Andy Hardy in* Love Laughs at Andy Hardy *(1946). His parents were still Lewis Stone and Fay Holden.*

'Varsity Drag.' Scriptwriters Betty Comden and Adolph Green, with Roger Edens, also supplied 'The French Lesson.' The film marked the directing debut of Charles Walters, who had previously been a choreographer for the Freed unit.

Green Dolphin Street (1947) was based on Elizabeth Goudge's romantic novel about the settlement of New Zealand and the Maori Wars. Lana Turner starred as the woman who travels to join her fiancée in New Zealand and later falls in love with the eccentric leader of the defense against the Maori (Van Johnson). The husband was played by Richard Hart, an actor the studio was grooming for stardom, but whose early promise was never fulfilled. Donna Reed had a brief role as Turner's sister who had been engaged to Hart, and goes into a convent when he sends for her sister by mistake.

The exotic scenes in New Zealand were intensified by a brilliantly effective tidal wave and earthquake which earned Academy Awards for the technicians in question, Arnold Gillespie and Warren Newcombe for visuals, and Douglas Shearer and Michael Steinore for sound.

Thanks to Turner's name, the public made it a hit. This was especially pleasing to the studio because the book had been the first winner of the M-G-M Novel Award, which carried a prize of $200,000.

In an unusual co-production deal, M-G-M and Praesens Film of Zürich collaborated on *The Search* (1948), a touching story of a lost and homeless German boy in a displaced persons camp in Switzerland. With the cooperation of the US Army, the film unit was allowed to shoot in the occupied zone of Germany.

The film starred Montgomery Clift as the American soldier who becomes involved in the boy's hunt for his family and helps the child through the necessary red tape before he is reunited with his mother, played by the opera singer Jarmila Novotna. Aline MacMahon played an officer with the International Refugee Organization, and the young boy was played by Ivan Jandl, who received a miniature Oscar for his efforts. Both Clift and director Fred Zinnemann were nominated, but the only other award was given to Richard Schweizter and David Wechsler who wrote the story and screenplay.

Movies about World War II had been made all through that conflict, and by 1948 interest had not waned. An unusual aspect of the war was portrayed in *Command Decision* (1948), based on the stage play by William Wister Haines. Director Sam Wood decided to stay with the successful format of the play, and there were very few action sequences. The plot concerned a series of bombing raids on a German aircraft factory from the point of view of the generals who order them.

Clark Gable starred, in his best post-war role, as the Air Force general trying to balance the necessity of the mission against the cost in human lives. Many of the critics found it stagey and talky, but praised the scene in which Gable talks down the only living member of a bomber crew. The cast also included Walter Pidgeon as Gable's superior, John Hodiak as the mission leader and Brian Donlevy as the General who replaces him after an investigation.

Arthur Freed's musical productions scored a double in 1948, with two films starring Judy Garland. The first was *The Pirate*, based on a straight play by S N Behrman which had starred the Lunts. It was set on a Caribbean island and the plot concerned a circus clown, Gene Kelly, who pretends to be a pirate to impress his lady love. Something of a send-up of the swashbuckling pictures of the thirties, it was definitely a Vincente Minnelli production in its total artificiality and stagey charm. Though the score was by Cole Porter, the only songs remembered are 'Be A Clown' and 'Mack the Black.'

Minnelli was so pleased with the teaming of Garland and Kelly that he cast them in his next musical, *Easter Parade* (1948). A few days into rehearsal, Kelly broke an ankle and was replaced by Fred Astaire. Today it is difficult to imagine anybody but Astaire in the role of the Broadway dancer who chooses Garland as his partner after the defection of Ann Miller.

Miller was also a replacement, hired when Cyd Charisse, who was originally cast as Nadine Hale, broke her leg. The

Opposite top: *Ivan Jandl (center) –* The Search *(1948).*
Opposite below: *John Hodiak, Walter Pidgeon, Van Johnson, Charles Bickford and Clark Gable starred in* Command Decision *(1948).*

Right: *'A Couple Of Swells' – Fred Astaire and Judy Garland in* Easter Parade *(1948).*
Below: *Gene Kelly, the circus clown in disguise, in pursuit of Judy Garland in* The Pirate *(1948).*

backstage story has always been helped by the insertion of musical numbers, and this was no exception. The 17 songs by Irving Berlin ran from 'Everybody's Doing It,' 'When the Midnight Choo Choo Leaves for Alabam,' 'Stepping Out With My Baby' to the famous title song. The showstopper, however, was 'A Couple of Swells' as Judy and Fred as a pair of hoboes mime their understanding of upper-class life. Judy's mimicry was terrific, her singing at its peak and she was matched perfectly with Astaire.

Without Judy Garland, there would have been no *Easter Parade*. Composer Irving Berlin wanted to do a show with her, and let Arthur Freed buy the rights to the song 'Easter Parade.' Freed then had his screenwriters Sidney Sheldon, Frances Goodrich and Albert Hackett write a story around it. The director was Charles Walters and reviews were spectacular. The public loved it, too, and it was the second-biggest box-office success of the year.

Nineteen forty-nine marked the 25th anniversary of the founding of M-G-M, and the studio celebrated with a tremendous lunch featuring the 80 stars and featured players then under contract. A subsequent publicity photo showed 58 of these stars, who ranged from June Allyson to Keenan Wynn, alphabetically, and included two Barrymores, Judy Garland and Lassie. Making the most of their past was one way to cover up for the present. Profits were up but the number and quality of films seemed to be down, as the New York Office and the Culver City Studio debated the way to turn.

One film with no problems at all was one of the first released in 1949. This was Mervyn Le Roy's adaptation of Louisa May Alcott's *Little Women*. The cast featured June Allyson as Jo, Janet Leigh as Meg, Margaret O'Brien as Beth and Elizabeth Taylor, in improbable golden curls, as Amy. Peter Lawford was Laurie and veteran actor Sir C Aubrey Smith played Laurie's grandfather in his final screen appearance at age 85.

The screenplay by Andrew Solt, Sarah Mason and Victor Heerman may have accentuated the sentimental side of the plot, but the performances were good, especially Allyson, who was unfortunately compared with Katharine Hepburn in the same role in the RKO Radio version of 1933. The exhibitors and box offices didn't care, and the jubilee year was off to a good start.

Nineteen-forty-nine was also the year that the English studio produced its first film since 1945 in the big new studio complex at Boreham Wood. The film was *Edward, My Son*, based on the Robert Morley-Noel Langley play about a ruthless self-made man whose demands on his son destroy the young man. The movie maintained the play's gimmick of not showing the title character, and lost the drama that a confrontation would have maintained. Deborah Kerr costarred as the man's neglected wife, and George Cukor directed.

A surprise hit of the year was *That Forsyte Woman* (1949), director Compton Bennett's version of the first book of John Galsworthy's *The Forsyte Saga*. It starred Greer Garson as Irene and Errol Flynn as an effective and affecting Soames, raising sympathy for a character caught by his own upbringing and lack of understanding.

In The Good Old Summertime (1949) was a remake of *The Shop Around The Corner* (1939) with music. It starred Van

Right: *Spencer Tracy played an unscrupulous self-made man in* Edward, My Son *(1949), here with Mervyn Johns.*
Opposite: *The four March girls, Amy (Elizabeth Taylor), Meg (Janet Leigh), Jo (June Allyson) and Beth (Margaret O'Brien) in* Little Women *(1949).*

Below: *The Forsytes including Soames (Errol Flynn) and Irene (Greer Garson) pose for a family portrait in* That Forsyte Woman *(1949).*

Johnson and Judy Garland as the antagonists who work in a music store run by S Z Sakall. The cast included Spring Byington, Buster Keaton and Clinton Sundberg as the other employees.

Her role as the salesgirl who sang, played the piano and sold sheet music gave Garland the opportunity to sing some wonderful old standards including 'I Don't Care' and 'Meet Me Tonight In Dreamland.' The director was Robert Z Leonard, but the film had the same wonderful idyllic feeling of the turn of the century that had made *Meet Me In St Louis* a hit. Garland and Minnelli's daughter Liza made her screen debut as Johnson and Garland's daughter in the finale.

A new head of production joined the studio in 1949. This was Dore Schary, who had been a screenwriter for several studios, including M-G-M, and had most recently headed RKO before he left following a disagreement with the owner, Howard Hughes. Schary brought several properties with him, and one was a war film called *Battleground*. Mayer was sure that by now people were tired of war movies, but Schary was just as sure the film would be a success.

Battleground (1949) was the story of a paratroop company hemmed in at Bastogne during the Battle of the Bulge in 1944. The film captured the locale, weather and tension of the situation and the cast, led by Van Johnson, was uniformly good, although the standout was James Whitmore, who received a nomination for Best Supporting Actor for his role as the veteran Sergeant Kinnie. The picture was nominated also, as was William Wellman, the director who had been responsible for some of the great hits of the thirties, including *Public Enemy* and *Nothing Sacred*. Awards were won by the screenplay by Robert Pirosh and the striking camerawork of Paul Vogel.

Schary had been correct. The public still wanted to see good war movies, and proved it by making *Battleground* the most profitable M-G-M picture of the year.

Above: *Van Johnson starred in* Battleground *(1949), a believable war film about the Battle of the Bulge.*
Opposite: *The musical* On The Town *(1949) featured Betty Garrett, Frank Sinatra, Ann Miller, Jules Munshin, Vera-Ellen and Gene Kelly.*

Left: In The Good Old Summertime *(1949) was a musical remake on* The Shop Around The Corner *(1939) starring S Z Sakall, Van Johnson and Judy Garland.*

The genesis of *On The Town* (1949) had been a ballet by Jerome Robbins, with music by Leonard Bernstein, called *Fancy Free*. In 1944, it became a Broadway show, with lyrics by Betty Comden and Adolph Green. Arthur Freed bought it, but was not able to start production for five years.

The plot was still basically the same as the ballet – three sailors in New York on a 24-hour leave. The sailors were Gene Kelly, who also directed, Frank Sinatra and Jules Munshin. The three ladies they pick up in the course of the day were Vera-Ellen as Miss Turnstiles, Betty Garrett as the cab driver Brunhilde Esterhazy and Ann Miller as Claire Huddeson, the anthropologist who captures Jules Munshin at the Museum of Natural History.

The brilliant original score by Bernstein was reduced, leaving only a few songs, including the wonderful number 'New York, New York' and some ballet music. Robbins' choreography was replaced with dances by Kelly and Stanley Donen.

The film never lets up from the exhilarating opening, as it moves about the city, stopping at many notable landmarks, including the New York Public Library and the Museum of Natural History where Ann Miller leads the rest of the cast through the prehistoric creatures in 'Prehistoric Man.' The Empire State Building is the scene of the exuberant title song.

Another popular musical was *The Barkleys of Broadway* (1949), which marked the reunion of Ginger Rogers and Fred Astaire after ten years. This happy occurrence was an accident, for Rogers was a replacement for Judy Garland, who had been scheduled to make the film with Astaire following her triumph the previous years in *Easter Parade*. Garland had been hospitalized for a nervous breakdown.

The Barkleys of Broadway was the story of a theatrical couple whose marriage is threatened when one of them wants to give up the musical stage in favor of serious drama. The movie included a wonderful reprise of 'They Can't Take That Away From Me,' which had been a high point of *Shall We Dance* (RKO-Radio, 1937). The other musical numbers included 'Manhattan Downbeat' and Fred's solo, 'Shoes With

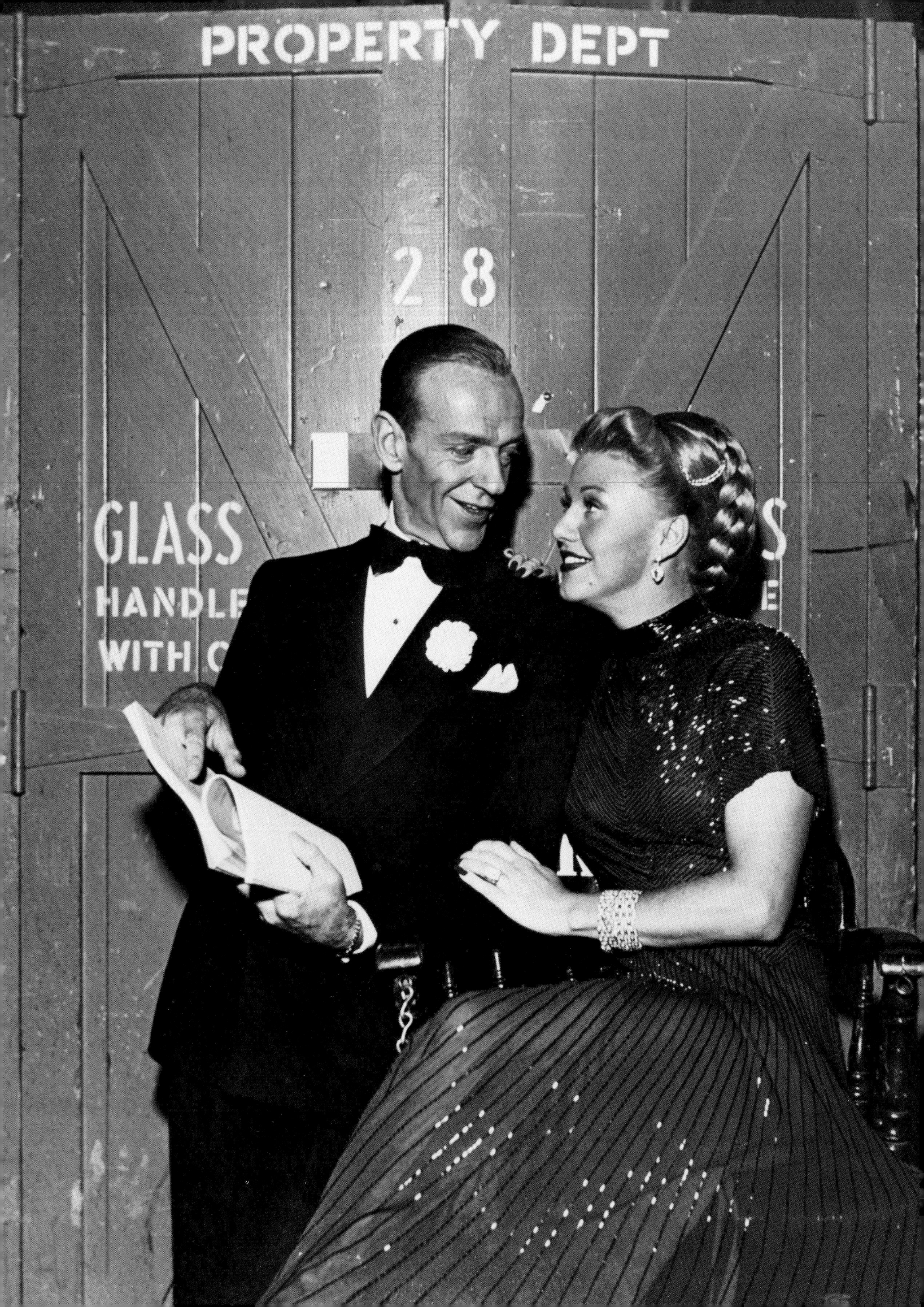
PROPERTY DEPT
28
GLASS
HANDLE
WITH

Opposite: *Fred Astaire and Ginger Rogers were reunited in* The Barkleys of Broadway *(1949).*

Right: *Claude Jarman Jr starred with Juano Hernandez in* Intruder in the Dust *(1949), as the white boy who is saved by a black, later accused of a white man's murder.*
Below: *Katharine Hepburn and Spencer Tracy had one of their greatest successes as the opposing lawyers in* Adam's Rib *(1949). Defendant Judy Holliday is in the witness box.*

Wings On,' which featured some wonderful trick photography. The screenplay was by Betty Comden and Adolph Green and Charles Walters directed for the Freed unit.

A total change of pace was *Intruder In the Dust* (1949), an adaptation of William Faulkner's novel about the near lynching of a black accused of a white man's murder in a Mississippi town. The director Clarence Brown had memories of the Atlanta Race riots at the turn of the century, and asked Mayer to let him do the picture as a favor.

Brown was one of the directors of longest standing at the studio, and had been Garbo's favorite, but he was also adept at comedy and action pictures. On Brown's advice, the film was shot on location in Oxford, Mississippi, Faulkner's

hometown, and used some 500 local residents. Its sympathetic treatment of the case, and the performances of Juano Hernandez, as the accused black Lucas Beauchamp, and Claude Jarman Jr, as the white boy who aids him, made it one of the most critically acclaimed of M-G-M's films of the forties.

A more popular film was another Spencer Tracy-Katharine Hepburn feature, *Adam's Rib* (1949), a courtroom comedy which pitted two married lawyers on opposite sides of an assault case. Hepburn played Amanda Bonner, the attorney for the defense of Doris Attinger (Judy Holliday) who had shot her husband Warren (Tom Ewell) when she found him in the arms of Jean Hagen. Tracy was Hepburn's husband, the prosecutor Adam Bonner.

The screenplay by Garson Kanin and Ruth Gordon was filled with witty comments on the battle of the sexes and women's equality. In the end Holliday is acquitted following Amanda's summing up: 'May it please the court, I submit that my entire line of defense is based on the proposition that persons of the female sex should be dealt with, before the law, as the equals of persons of the male sex. I submit that I cannot hope to argue this line before minds hostile to and prejudiced against the female sex.'

The entire cast was good, but Holliday was outstanding as the dumb wife who fortunately is a bad shot. She won the Academy Award for best supporting actress, but for her performance in *Born Yesterday*. Director George Cukor experimented with long takes which proved effective in the scenes between the principals.

Tracy's next film was *Father of The Bride* (1950), a delightful comedy based on the novel by Edward Streeter. Tracy played Stanley T Banks, a part originally meant for Jack Benny, whose daughter Kay (Elizabeth Taylor) throws the house in an uproar of wedding arrangements when she announces her engagement to Buckley Dunstan (Don Taylor). After months of preparations, which involve lovely sequences of the Banks meeting the groom's parents (Billie Burke and Moroni Olsen) and consultations about the dress and catering, as well as a scene where Tracy encourages the hesitant bride to go through with it, the wedding takes place.

Ably assisted by Joan Bennett as his wife, Tracy was marvelous as the man pushed aside by the problems a wedding entails. The director, Vincente Minnelli, may have idealized his typical American family, but the public didn't care and the movie was so popular that M-G-M followed it with a sequel, *Father's Little Dividend* (1951) with the same cast.

A prestige production of 1950 was *The Magnificent Yankee* with Louis Calhern playing the part of Justice Oliver Wendell Holmes as he had for three years on the stage. Adapted by Emmett Lavery from his own play, *The Magnificent Yankee* traced the career of Justice Holmes from his arrival in Washington during Theodore Roosevelt's administration, to his retirement 30 years later at the age of 87.

Ann Harding played Fanny Holmes, and Eduard Franz and Philip Ober were featured as Owen Wister and Justice Brandeis. The director was John Sturges, who was later one of the directors on the strange M-G-M episodic experiment, *It's A Big Country*.

Calhern also appeared as Buffalo Bill Cody in the M-G-M version of *Annie Get Your Gun* (1950), replacing Frank Morgan, who died during production at the age of 60. But that was not the only replacement in the film. Star Judy Garland suffered another breakdown, and the role of Annie Oakley was given to Betty Hutton. Director George Sidney replaced Charles Walters who had replaced Busby Berkeley.

The plot traced the rise to stardom of Annie Oakley, the featured sharpshooter of Buffalo Bill's Wild West Show and her romance with another marksman, Frank Butler of Pawnee Bill's, when they meet in Cincinnati where both shows are playing. In the end, the two shows merge and Annie marries Frank.

Annie marked the M-G-M debut of Howard Keel, who played Frank Butler, a part which used his wonderful singing voice to advantage. Veteran actor J Carrol Naish played Sitting Bull and Edward Arnold was Pawnee Bill.

The score by Irving Berlin contained wonderful numbers like 'Doin' What Comes Naturally,' 'The Girl That I Marry,' 'Anything You Can Do,' 'They Say It's Wonderful' and the show-stopping 'There's No Business Like Show Business,' which was used as the finale complete with trick shooting, fancy riding and a vast chorus of cowboys and Indians.

The success of *Annie Get Your Gun* was overwhelming. The production difficulties were forgotten and the studio basked in its triumph. They also began planning for more musicals – both Broadway hits and Hollywood originals.

Another type of film also had a revival. The big adventure film had lost its impact after the war, but M-G-M brought it back with a bang. *King Solomon's Mines* (1950) was an adaptation of H Rider Haggard's best-known novel about the Great White Hunter Allan Quartermain. Haggard's original sent Quartermain, Sir Henry Curtin and Captain Goode into unexplored territory for priceless treasure. Helen Deutsch's screenplay sent Quartermain, Elizabeth Curtin and her brother into unexplored territory to find the husband she was estranged from. Of course, she and Quartermain fall in

Opposite far left: *Elizabeth Taylor as Kay and Spencer Tracy as Stanley Banks, the* Father of The Bride *(1950).*
Left: The Magnificent Yankee *(1950), starred Ann Harding as* Fanny and Louis Calhern as Justice Holmes.
Below: *Howard Keel and Betty Hutton in 'There's No Business Like Show Business,' the finale of* Annie Get Your Gun *(1950).*

love, but the discovery of her husband's body when they are trapped within the fabled mines leads to a happy ending.

Stewart Granger had a marvelous time as the ideal hunter. Deborah Kerr as Mrs Curtin was a perfect foil, whether cutting her hair after the loss of her last hairpin, or being rudely awakened by a large snake sliding through her tent. Her brother was played by Richard Carlson, who managed to maintain his presence before the fireworks of the other principals. A Watusi named Siriaque played the mysterious native Umbopa who turns out to be the king whose throne has been usurped by a treacherous cousin.

The photography by Robert Surtees was outstanding, taking advantage of the African terrain and fauna, pausing to admire an ant hill or back away from a hunting leopard. But there were also wonderful Watusi dances, a battle with spears for the throne and a frighteningly realistic bush fire which starts a stampede.

The resultant film footage was so vast that M-G-M adapted another Haggard novel into a film called *Watusi* (1959) to use up some of the *King Solomon's Mines* outtakes. *Drums of Africa* (1963) also used much of the same footage, but neither could compare with the original.

Summer Stock (1950) found Judy Garland running a boarding house for actors while her sister Gloria de Haven was playing the lead in the barn theater. Of course, Judy has to take over de Haven's part at the last moment, and saves the show. In the finale, filmed after the rest of the film was completed, she proved that all the old talent was there as she belted out 'Get Happy.' It was her last M-G-M film. Emotional problems led to a cancellation of her contract and a redistribution of her roles.

One of the films scheduled for Garland was *Royal Wedding* (1950) which would have teamed her once more with Fred Astaire. Her role went to Jane Powell. Powell and Astaire played a brother-and-sister dance team in London at the time of the wedding of the Princess Elizabeth to Prince Philip. He falls in love with Sarah Churchill, and she with Peter Lawford. Besides singing the song with the longest title to date. 'How Could You Believe Me When I Say I Love You When You Know I've Been A Liar All My Life,' Fred had a magnificent dance sequence up the walls and across the ceiling of his room. It was later revealed that this was accomplished by mounting the box that was the room set on a hydraulic pivot that allowed the room to turn. Stanley Donen directed in his first solo effort, and the book and lyrics were by Alan Jay Lerner, with music by Burton Lane.

Opposite top: *Kimursi, Richard Carlson, Deborah Kerr and Stewart Granger are awakened by a leopard attack during the night in* King Solomon's Mines *(1950).*
Opposite below: *Judy Garland sings 'Get Happy' in* Summerstock *(1950), her last film for M-G-M.*

Right: *Jane Powell and Fred Astaire as the brother and sister song-and-dance team in* Royal Wedding *(1950).*

Left: *Louis Calhern as the venal lawyer Emmerich and Sam Jaffe as the safecracker Doc Riedenscheider enjoy the results of their crime in* The Asphalt Jungle *(1950).*
Opposite top: *Mario Lanza as Enrico Caruso sings the* Brindisi *from* Cavalleria Rusticana *in* The Great Caruso *(1951).*

Opposite below: *The* Cotton Blossom *comes to town in* Showboat *(1951).*
Below: *Peter Ustinov as the Emperor Nero attends the games in* Quo Vadis *(1951).*

The Asphalt Jungle (1950) was a different crime picture, contrasting the criminals who actually carried out the meticulously planned robbery and the venal well-educated lawyer who planned the crime. The detailed recounting of the burglary was part of its fascination, but the characters were equally noteworthy. Louis Calhern played the lawyer, who puts himself above the law and takes advantage of it.

The gang was led by Sam Jaffe as 'Doc' Riedenscheider, the mastermind and expert appraiser, and his confederates included Sterling Hayden as the lookout, Anthony Caruso as the explosives expert, James Whitmore as the getaway car driver and Marc Lawrence as the money man. Also appearing were Marilyn Monroe as Calhern's mistress and Jean Hagen as Hayden's girl friend.

The robbery was merely the lead in to the true conflict which was established when Calhern begins his double-crossing plot. And then the film follows each member of the gang as he is apprehended or killed.

The script by John Huston, who also directed, was taut and well-paced and nominated for the best screenplay of 1950. Sam Jaffe was also in the running for best supporting actor.

One of the biggest films of 1951 was *Quo Vadis*, the first sound version of Henryk Sienkiewicz's novel about Christians in Nero's Rome. The film was made at the vast Cinecittà studio outside Rome where it now was cheaper to make a movie that required 5000 extras in one scene. At the outset, the stars were Gregory Peck and Elizabeth Taylor and the director John Huston, but six months later Robert Taylor and Deborah Kerr were the leads and Mervyn Le Roy was in the director's chair.

The story of *Quo Vadis* is the romance between the Christian girl Ligia and the Roman officer Marcus Vinicius, who finally come together at the games where Christians are thrown to the lions, and Ligia faces a mad bull. The bull is killed by her faithful slave Ursus, and the populace demands that the Emperor Nero free the Christians. Nero's bodyguard join the revolt, and Nero commits suicide.

The role of Nero was played by Peter Ustinov, who had a

field day as the Emperor, plucking his lyre while the city goes up in flames, submitting his guests to poetry readings of his own execrable verse and flying into a temper tantrum when crossed. Also appearing were Patricia Laffen as the cruel empress Poppaea, Finlay Currie as St Peter, Abraham Sofaer as St Paul and Buddy Baer as the faithful Ursus.

The script, by John Lee Mahin, S N Behrman and Sonya Levien, had been the subject of much discussion between Mayer and Schary, as Mayer wanted a straight adaptation while Schary favored a political slant comparing Nero to Mussolini. It didn't matter. Any political aspects would have gone straight over the head of the audience who went for the spectacle and the drama. The tremendous initial cost of $7,000,000 was quickly regained when the film grossed over $12,000,000.

Mario Lanza made two pictures *The Midnight Kiss* (1949) and *The Toast of New Orleans* (1950) before *The Great Caruso* (1951), a romanticized biography of the immortal tenor. It was the perfect vehicle for the new M-G-M star, and the production even had the blessing of the singer's widow, who wrote the biographical framework.

The plot was slight as it followed the young singer from Naples to a triumphal career at the Metropolitan, but the film gave Lanza a chance to sing 27 numbers, including nine operatic excerpts from operas like *Aida, Tosca, Rigoletto* and *Cavalleria Rusticana* with such divas as Jarmila Novotna, Dorothy Kirsten, Blanche Thebom and Lucine Amara. The film even had a hit song, 'The Loveliest Night of the Year.' based on a Viennese waltz, 'Over the Waves.'

Another well received musical offering was *Show Boat* (1951) starring Howard Keel and Kathryn Grayson. The Jerome Kern-Oscar Hammerstein II musical had opened on Broadway in 1929, and been an instant success. Universal had made two film versions (in 1929 and 1936), but Arthur Freed felt the world was ready for a brand new one in Technicolor.

Kathryn Grayson as Magnolia and Howard Keel as Gaylord were perfectly matched. The part of the mulatto Julie had been scheduled for Judy Garland, but after her departure was played by Ava Gardner, and very well too. Her songs were dubbed by Annette Warren, although oddly enough,

Gardner did the singing on the soundtrack recording, which was also popular. It is a pity that M-G-M did not cast Lena Horne in the part since she had done a magnificent job with two of the songs in *Till The Clouds Roll By* (1946). Also in the cast were Joe E Brown as Cap'n Andy, Agnes Moorehead as Parthy and Marge and Gower Champion as Ellie and Frank.

Show Boat owes much of its continued popularity to the score, which features such wonderful songs as 'Why Do I Love You,' 'Make Believe,' 'Can't Help Lovin' That Man Of Mine' and the unforgettable 'Old Man River.' The 1951 M-G-M production also included 'You Are Love,' 'Life Upon The Wicked Stage' and 'After the Ball,' a popular song of the 1890s.

The most acclaimed movie of 1951 was definitely *An American In Paris*. The story by Alan Jay Lerner told of a GI who stays in Paris after the war to see if he can succeed as an artist. The cast was headed by Gene Kelly and had only four other principals, Nina Foch as a predatory woman who is less interested in Kelly's art than in Kelly, Oscar Levant as a wisecracking American pianist, Georges Guetary as a French singer and a new discovery, Leslie Caron, as Kelly's love interest.

The story was actually built around the Gershwin music which included songs like 'I'll Build A Staircase To Paradise,' sung by Guetary, 'Our Love Is Here To Stay,' 'I Got Rhythm,' a charming number danced by Kelly and a dozen or so small children, 'S'Wonderful' and two instrumental pieces the 'Concerto in F' (Third movement only) and the tone poem,

'An American in Paris,' which provides the music for the climactic ballet.

The ballet was a sticking point. The New York office, after screening rushes, felt that the film was complete. The director Vincente Minnelli, the producer Arthur Freed, the choreographer and star Gene Kelly and the writer Alan Jay Lerner all believed that the ballet was a necessary part of the film. They convinced Mayer, who okayed the cost (which was $400,000). It was one of his last acts as head of the M-G-M Studio.

The ballet sequence, which runs for 18 minutes, is an imaginative tribute to the city of Paris and the artists like Toulouse-Lautrec and Raoul Dufy who have painted her. It is the highlight of the film, and Alan Lerner, for one, wondered if the film would have survived without it.

The film won a total of eight Academy Awards, including best picture, best screenplay and best scoring. The Irving Thalberg Production Award was presented to Arthur Freed and Kelly was honored with a special Oscar for his choreography. Also honored was the art direction team headed by Cedric Gibbons, who had created Paris out of three street sets on the back lot and a brilliant use of miniatures and rear projection.

The Red Badge of Courage (1951) was a different story. From its inception, the film had been a bone of contention in the M-G-M offices. Mayer was sure that the public was tired of war movies, and that after World War II, wouldn't be interested in the Civil War anyway. Schary, on the other hand, was determined to film the classic, and went to the New York office for backing.

Stephen Crane's novel set in the Civil War about a young boy's coming of age in battle was lovingly adapted and directed by John Huston. The film starred Audie Murphy as the young boy, and featured a good cast including Bill Mauldin, Douglas Dick, John Dierkes and Royal Dano.

Problems arose when the Production Code found some of the language ('hell,' 'damn,' 'fer Gawd's sake') unacceptable. Following the usual audience previews, stringent cuts were ordered of the more graphic battle scenes and a narration by James Whitmore was added in the hope of diminishing apparent audience confusion.

The film received good notices, many citing its fidelity to the novel and calling the film a classic, but it didn't have the necessary audience response, and M-G-M did not feel that they could afford to make too many pictures for prestige.

One of the results of the film was to increase the enmity between Schary and Mayer. They came to loggerheads again over the employment of actors under suspicion of the House Committee on Un-American Activities.

Eventually Mayer handed the head office of Loew's Inc. in New York an ultimatum. They would have to choose between him and Schary. New York seemed to take into consideration only the improvement in economic returns since Schary had joined M-G-M in 1949, and went with Schary. Mayer resigned after 27 years as the studio head of M-G-M. Hollywood had changed and the studio system was changing too.

Opposite: An American In Paris *(1951):*
Top: *Gene Kelly and Georges Guetary do a number on a Paris streetcorner.*
Below: *Gene Kelly and Leslie Caron in the ballet at the end of the film.*

Right: The Red Badge of Courage *(1951) starring Audie Murphy (with flag), was a critical success, but not a popular one.*

THE
SILVER
AGE

WHEN DORE SCHARY BECAME head of the M-G-M studio, one of the local wags remarked 'it was like becoming mayor of Rome while it was burning.' It was felt that it would be impossible to re-establish the old magnificence in the old way. Changes would have to be made.

Schary felt that the studio was first of all overburdened by its overhead. There were some 4000 employees making an average of 29 pictures a year. The studio would either have to make more movies or cut down on the staff as part of a rigid system of economy. An additional problem was the growing popularity of television. Audiences would not go to the movies to see something similar to that on their own screens. Only exceptional films were making any money. There would have to be a change in the studio's policy towards its stars. As their contracts lapsed, stars were let go or given a contract for a single year.

The films that were released soon after Schary's takeover showed no sign of this belt-tightening. One of the highpoints of 1952 was the release of *Singin' In The Rain*, a loving valentine to the movie industry at the time of the conversion to sound in the late twenties.

The plot followed vaudevillians Don Lockwood (Gene Kelly) and Cosmo Brown (Donald O'Connor) into the early movies, where Don rises from stunt man to star. He is then teamed with the lovely, but vacuous Lina Lamont (Jean Hagen), but off the set he is dating a pretty starlet, Kathy Selden (Debbie Reynolds). The advent of sound takes the studio by surprise, and there is a marvelous sequence with the new microphones picking up every sound available from voices to the slap of a fan and the rustle of taffeta, all amplified. Another problem is Lina's voice, which like some real

Opposite top: *Gene Kelly in love and* Singin' In The Rain *(1952).*
Opposite below: *Donald O'Connor, Debbie Reynolds and Gene Kelly sing 'Good Morning' in* Singin' In The Rain *(1952).*

Previous spread: *Miss Sarah Brown of the Save-A-Soul Mission (Jean Simmons) and Sky Masterson (Marlon Brando) in* Guys and Dolls *(1955).*
Right: *Stewart Granger enters Eleanor Parker's dressing room in* Scaramouche *(1952).*

stars of the period, does not match her appearance. After an all-night session following a terrible preview, Don, Cosmo and Kathy have invented dubbing. The film in question, which was laughed at during the preview, is now enthusiastically applauded and it is revealed that Kathy did the voice-over for Lina.

Most of the songs, 'All I Do Is Dream Of You,' 'Singin' in the Rain,' 'I've Got A Feeling You're Fooling' and 'You Were Meant For Me,' actually came from the era in question, and had been written by the producer Arthur Freed when he was merely a member of the M-G-M music department. One song, 'Make 'Em Laugh,' Freed and his old partner Nacio Herb Brown wrote especially for the production. It was near enough to Cole Porter's 'Be A Clown' to raise eyebrows, though Porter politely said nothing about it. It was a wonderful solo for Donald O'Connor however, allowing him to get hit by a plank, walk into a wall, wrestle with several dummies and lose control of his facial muscles. The number was so strenuous that it put O'Connor in the hospital for three days on completion. When he was released it was discovered that the film had been ruined in processing, and O'Connor had to perform it all over again, even to the stay in the hospital.

The film finishes with 'Broadway Ballet' a triumphal great dance number describing Kelly's own rise to stardom, which includes an intriguing encounter with a seductive vamp, Cyd Charisse, made up to look like the twenties screen siren, Louise Brooks.

Even in 1952, the M-G-M studio was still staffed by many technicians and other personnel whose stories and memories obviously gave *Singin' In The Rain* an air of believability beyond the fun and laughter. One of these was Cedric Gibbons, the art director, who had actually begun his

career in the movies at Thomas Edison's studio in 1914 before moving to Goldwyn and then to M-G-M.

Singin' In The Rain was even more popular than Kelly's two preceding films, *On The Town* and *An American In Paris*, but oddly enough received only one Academy Award nomination which went to Jean Hagen as best supporting actress for her brilliant caricature of the silent movie star.

Casting back to the twenties had reminded the studio of a number of films that were probably right for revision. One of these was *Scaramouche* (1952) which had first seen the light of day in 1923 with Ramon Novarro and Lewis Stone in the leads. The swashbuckling novel by Rafael Sabatini was thought to be the perfect vehicle for Stewart Granger, so Ronald Miller and George Froeschel rewrote the original screenplay by Rex Ingram.

Scaramouche is the tale of Andre Moreau, a young man in pre-revolutionary France who discovers that his father had been an important noble. He also believes that Aline de Gavrillac, the girl he has fallen in love with, is thus his half-sister. She is being courted by a nobleman, the Marquis de Maynes, who picks a fight and kills Andre's best friend. Andre tries to avenge him, but is badly beaten by de Maynes who has the reputation of being the finest swordsman in all France. He vows revenge and seeks out de Maynes' fencing master for instruction while he is in hiding, masquerading as Scaramouche, a member of a theatrical troupe. One day, finding de Maynes in the audience, Andre challenges him to a duel and beats him, though he finds he cannot kill him. This makes sense in light of a revelation from his friend's father, that it is De Maynes' father who was Andre's also and thus he is free to marry the girl he loves.

The high point of the film was definitely the six-and-a-half

minute duel between Granger, as Scaramouche, and Mel Ferrer as de Maynes. In reality, a duel of this length would be an impossibility, but as fantasy, the fury and duration of the duel are a treasure, as the opponents fight their way about the theater, through the boxes, over the seats and onto the stage. Granger was one of the finest duelists at M-G-M, and had studied with Jean Heremans, a Belgian fencing champion. Mel Ferrer also handled his sword and role with grace, and the right touch of evil.

Others in the cast included Janet Leigh as the lovely Aline, Richard Anderson as Andre's friend Philippe and Lewis Stone, who had played de Maynes in the 1923 version, as Philippe's father. The director was George Sidney.

A surprise hit of 1952 was *Million Dollar Mermaid* with M-G-M's star swimmer Esther Williams as Annette Kellerman, the Australian whose swimming talent had eventually brought her to Hollywood, where she rocked that rather provincial town in 1920 with her one-piece bathing suit.

Like all of Williams' movies it was remarkably popular and included more of the wonderful water ballets and acrobatic sequences of her earlier efforts, *Pagan Love Song* (1950) and *Neptune's Daughter* (1949). The cast included Victor Mature, Walter Pidgeon and ballerina Maria Tallchief as Pavlova. The director was Mervyn LeRoy.

Following her great debut in *An American in Paris*, the

126

Opposite top: Million Dollar Mermaid *(1952), starring Esther Williams, included several fantastic water ballets.*
Right: *Robert Taylor (right) in the attack on Torquilstone Castle in* Ivanhoe *(1952).*

Opposite below: *Leslie Caron played a homeless orphan in* Lili *(1952), Mel Ferrer played the puppeteer who falls in love with her.*

studio searched for another property for Leslie Caron. Eventually they settled on a Paul Gallico story about a French orphan who falls in love with a crippled puppeteer in a traveling circus. It was called *Lili* (1952). Like *An American In Paris, Lili* included a ballet with the puppets, now lifesize to showcase the real talent of Miss Caron, who had been discovered by Gene Kelly at the Ballets des Champs Elysees in Paris.

Others in the cast included Mel Ferrer as the puppeteer, as well as Jean Pierre Aumont, Zsa Zsa Gabor and Kurt Kasznar. The screenplay was by Helen Deutsch. The picture was nominated for several awards, although the only category that won was the score by Bronislau Kaper. The enchanting and popular song, 'Hi Lili, Hi Lo' did not even receive a nomination.

In the 1960s the story became the base of the successful musical *Carnival*, by Jerry Herman, one of the rare occurrences when the Broadway stage borrowed from Hollywood.

The M-G-M studio in England at Boreham Wood, had continued to turn out small budget movies without much interference from Culver City, and by 1952 there was a nice backlog of profits that could not be taken out of the country due to currency restrictions. Schary had the brilliant idea to make a major film in England to make use of these funds. The film would be distributed world-wide, of course, and bring some of the profits back to the head office. For this project, Schary chose Sir Walter Scott's *Ivanhoe*, a tale of the Third Crusade that would demand lavish production values and vast sets.

Scott's novel had never been filmed before, though its plot, which combines knight errant, fair maidens, tournaments, Robin Hood and the Military Order of the Knights Templar, seemed like a natural. Robert Taylor was cast as Ivanhoe, with Joan Fontaine as Rowena and Elizabeth Taylor as Rebecca. Rebecca is the daughter of the Jewish merchant Isaac of York, who rescues Ivanhoe when he is wounded at a tournament. George Sanders costarred as the evil Templar Brian de Bois Guilbert (described by the author himself as an 'unprincipled voluptuary'), who captures Rowena, Rebecca and most of the cast and holds them in his castle until they are freed by Ivanhoe and Robin Hood and his Merry Men. Meanwhile Bois Guilbert has escaped with Rebecca who he threatens to denounce as a witch if she does not yield to him. She won't, and is about to go to the stake when Ivanhoe arrives as her champion to challenge Bois Guilbert in a duel to the death. Bois Guilbert is killed, still declaring his love for Rebecca, and Rowena and Ivanhoe are reunited.

The cast included many great British character actors such as Finlay Currie, Felix Aylmer, Emlyn Williams, Basil Sydney and Valentine Dyall. The tournaments and battle scenes are wonderfully played out. The film, which opened at Radio City Music Hall, was a smash hit, and Schary made plans to produce more medieval spectaculars at Boreham Wood. The next was *Knights of the Round Table* (1954) based on Malory's *Le Morte D'Arthur*, again with Robert Taylor, to be followed by *Quentin Durward* (1955) in which Taylor costarred with Kay Kendall.

The Band Wagon (1953) started life as a revue in 1931 starring Fred and Adele Astaire. It surfaced again in 1949 as *Dancing in the Dark* (Twentieth Century-Fox). Minnelli and his writers, Adolph Green and Betty Comden, took the title and the wonderful score, and added a new screenplay, which was a sophisticated version of the old 'let's put on a show' concept.

Fred Astaire starred as Tony Hunter, a Hollywood star attempting a Broadway comeback in a revue at the sug-

gestion of his writing friends Nanette Fabray and Oscar Levant. The director is to be the great classical actor-director Jack Buchanan, and a young dancer Cyd Charisse is hired as the female lead. The original show as conceived by Buchanan is too artistic and lays an egg, literally. Fred, Cyd and the others persuade him to make changes, liven it up, take it on the road and bring it back for a triumphant opening, or rather finale. 'That's Entertainment.'

The score featured a number of wonderful numbers including Nanette leading the chorus in 'Louisiana Hayride,' Fred's slightly melancholy, 'By Myself,' which segues into the joyous 'Got A Shine On My Shoes,' and Fred and Jack's debonair duet, 'I Guess I'll Have To Change My Plans.' Other showstoppers were the lovely 'Dancing in the Dark' by Cyd and Fred, the elaborate 'Girl Hunt' ballet and the never to be forgotten 'Triplets,' in which Fred, Jack and Nanette, dressed up as babies, informed the audience that 'M-G-M has got a Leo/But Mama has got a trio.' That's Entertainment, indeed.

M-G-M had not tackled Shakespeare since the elaborate production of *Romeo and Juliet* in 1936, but under the new

administration of Dore Schary, director Joseph L Mankiewicz and producer John Houseman, made *Julius Caesar* (1953). Both men had in mind a version that would reflect the recent rise and fall of a dictator, but felt they also had a better structure for such opinions than *Quo Vadis* had been.

The film followed the continuity of the play, with some cuts in the fashion that had made Olivier's *Henry V* (GB 1945) so powerful. John Gielgud starred as Cassius and James Mason was a magnificent Brutus. Louis Calhern appeared in the title role with Greer Garson as his wife Calpurnia and Deborah Kerr as Brutus' wife Portia. The unexpected casting of Marlon Brando as Marc Antony gave the film one of its more memorable performances. Brando had studied the art of speaking Shakespeare with Gielgud, and proved that he could be a fine classical actor, when he wished.

Producer Houseman remembers that the speeches would not allow for the normal movie convention of cutting away to the silent observer for reaction during a long speech, and thus the film developed its own sense of rhythm. It was also felt that shooting the film in black and white would add to the intensity and sense of tragedy.

A later remake in color starring Jason Robards and Charleton Heston proved them correct. The remake was also harmed by the inability of Robards, an actor second to none in most cases, to understand the music inherent in Shakespeare's plays.

Opposite: *Fred Astaire and Cyd Charisse in the Girl Hunt Ballet, a take-off on the hard-boiled detective novels of Mickey Spillane, in* The Band Wagon *(1953).*

Below: *'The Ides of March have come.' 'Aye, Caesar, but not gone.' Louis Calhern as Julius Caesar, Morgan Farley as Artemidorus, John Gielgud as Cassius –* Julius Caesar *(1953).*

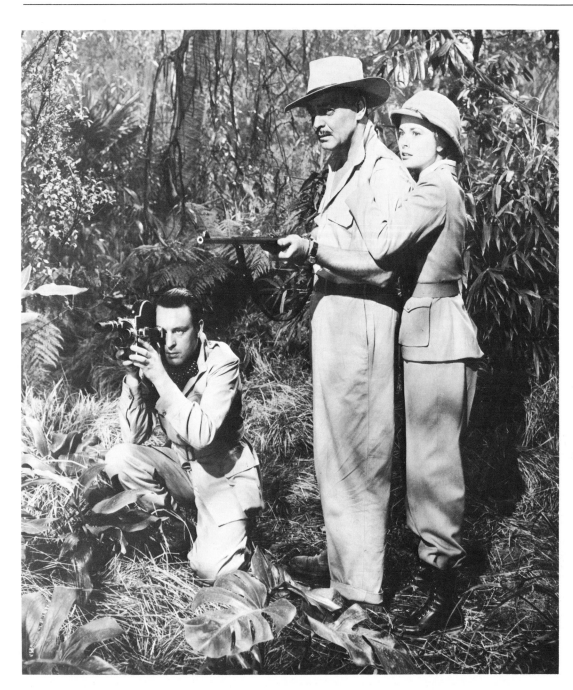

Clark Gable, who had made a series of rather depressing westerns and adventures since *Command Decision*, came back to the top of his form in *Mogambo* (1953) a remake of *Red Dust*, although the scene had been transferred to Africa. Gable plays a great white hunter who becomes involved with the wife of a client. Also present on the safari is Eloise Kelly, an American showgirl, played by Ava Gardner, a transformation of the role originated by Harlow. The Mary Astor role of the wife was given to a stunning newcomer, Grace Kelly. Donald Sinden played her husband.

The director was John Ford, and the cinematography by Robert Surtees was as brilliant as that he produced for *King Solomon's Mines* (1950). The conflict between Kelly and Gable, and Gable and Gardner, made the movie a box-office hit.

Shakespeare was given an entirely different treatment in *Kiss Me Kate* (1953), an adaptation of the Cole Porter hit, based on *The Taming Of The Shrew*. The play-within-a-play structure was retained, as the screenplay, like the Broadway show, set Shakespeare's *Shrew* within the context of a theater production, dwelling on the conflicts, emotional and otherwise, among the cast.

Howard Keel was magnificent as Petruchio, and Kathryn Grayson was his Kate. Ann Miller played Bianca, offstage and on, and had a wonderful routine with Bobby Van, Bob Fosse and Tommy Rall in 'Tom, Dick or Harry.' For many, the best number was 'Brush Up Your Shakespeare,' sung by James Whitmore and Keenan Wynn as the two hoods who are putting the squeeze on Bobby Van for his gambling debts.

The witty Cole Porter lyrics were occasionally cleaned up, or lost in the background of a scene. The lovely soliloquy, 'I Am Ashamed That Women Are So Simple,' was again spoken rather than sung. Another curious note was the sets for 'the play', which were the last word in contemporary for the 1950s, and consequently have dated much more than the rest of the film.

Other songs from the Broadway show included 'Too Darn Hot,' 'Why Can't You Behave,' 'So In Love' and 'Wunderbar.'

The following year M-G-M brought out an original musical, *Seven Brides For Seven Brothers* (1954). It was based on a short story by Stephen Vincent Benet with a score by Gene de Paul and Johnny Mercer. It starred Howard Keel as the eldest of seven brothers who decides their lives need some civilizin', so he takes a wife, Jane Powell. At first appalled by the idea

Opposite: *Donald Sinden, Clark Gable and Grace Kelly in* Mogambo *(1953).*
Above: *The Barn-Raising ballet, with choreography by Michael Kidd, was one of the highlights of* Seven Brides For Seven Brothers *(1954).*

Right: *The play within a play – Kathryn Grant as Kate and Howard Keel as Petruchio enjoy married life. James Whitmore and Keenan Wynn (far right) keep an eye on both in* Kiss Me Kate *(1953).*

of being the only maid to seven slobs, she soon has them clean and minding their manners. She also takes them to a barn raising where for the first time they meet the available young girls in the district. The barn raising turns into a fight among the other young swains of the district over the girls, and the brothers return home smitten. Comes the winter, and egged on by their married brother, they head for town and abduct the girls, bringing them back to the remote farm, after closing the pass to town with an avalanche. The wife is furious, takes the girls under her wing and banishes all seven brothers to the barn. The husband takes off to his hunting cabin in a fury.

By spring, matters have eased somewhat, due in part to the imminent arrival of the wife's baby. When the snow in the pass has cleared, and a posse from the town arrives at the farm, the girls are ready to stay, and are allowed to do so when they all claim the crying baby as their own. A mass wedding follows.

The gentle plot, in a screenplay by Albert Hackett, Frances Goodrich and Dorothy Kingsley, was given a wit and impudence that was matched by the score which features several lovely songs, including 'Bless Your Beautiful Hide,' 'Wonderful, Wonderful Day,' 'When You're In Love' and 'Goin' Courtin',' but the best number by far was the wonderful barn raising number which featured inspired choreography by Michael Kidd and was brilliantly performed by such classically trained dancers as Jacques d'Amboise and Matt Mattox, as well as Jeff Richards, Russ Tamblyn, Tommy Rall and Marc Platt. At once athletic and graceful, this ballet refuted the idea that dancing was for sissies. Once again Stanley Donen had created a musical hit.

A surprise hit of 1954 was one of Schary's own productions, *Bad Day At Black Rock*, starring Spencer Tracy as the one-armed war veteran searching for the Japanese father of a dead war hero to deliver the son's posthumous medal. The picture begins with an introduction to the town of Black Rock, which is so small the train doesn't even stop there regularly, but does one day to let Tracy off. Searching for the hero's father, he encounters a great deal of hostility and no help. Eventually he discovers that some of the townspeople were responsible for the death of the old Japanese and the subsequent burning of his farm. Before he leaves, the killers have paid for their crime and the old man is avenged.

Director John Sturges made this one of the most suspenseful movies ever filmed, as the stories of both Tracy and the crime are revealed. The cast included Robert Ryan, Dean Jagger, Ernest Borgnine and Lee Marvin, who gave a remarkable performance as one of the small-town louts.

Grace Kelly made another stir in a adventure set in the emerald mines of Colombia, *Green Fire* (1954), costarring Stewart Granger. Director Andrew Marton, who had been partly responsible for *King Solomon's Mines*, took a similar-sized crew to South America to film this story of a miner who finally strikes it rich, and wins the girl after a terrible flood had destroyed his emerald field.

Another Broadway musical to be produced by M-G-M in 1953 was *Brigadoon*, the Alan Jay Lerner-Frederick Loewe fantasy about a Scottish village that appears only once every hundred years. Gene Kelly and Van Johnson starred as the two Americans who come upon it, and Cyd Charisse played the girl Kelly falls in love with. The songs, including 'The Heather On The Hill,' 'Almost Like Being In Love' and 'There But For You Go I,' were lovely, but for once the production by Arthur Freed and the direction by Vincente Minnelli was strained, although the box office returns were very profitable.

Also profitable were those from an absorbing revelation of boardroom politics, *Executive Suite* (1954). In one of the last M-G-M all-star productions, director Robert Wise brought together Dean Jagger, Louis Calhern, Fredric March, William

Opposite: *John J MacReedy (Spencer Tracy) checks in to the hotel in* Bad Day At Black Rock *(1954). John Ericson is behind the desk.*

Right: *Paul Douglas and Stewart Granger discover emeralds in* Green Fire *(1954).*

Below: *Gene Kelly and Van Johnson, two lost Americans, arrive in a mysterious Scottish village in* Brigadoon *(1953).*

Gene Kelly appeared once again in *It's Always Fair Weather* (1955) with Michael Kidd and Dan Dailey as three reunited war buddies. Despite the undisputed talent of all concerned (as usual the script was by Comden and Green, the producer was Arthur Freed and Stanley Donen shared the directing with Kelly), the old magic was missing. *It's Always Fair Weather* did have a wonderful dance sequence, with Kelly on roller skates, entitled 'She Likes Me (I Like Myself),' as well as the magical opening number which takes the three friends dancing all over New York at night, in and out of cabs, and for one inspired moment with garbage can lids on their feet. It was the last of the Kelly/Donen collaborations, and Donen left M-G-M to become an independent producer.

Guys and Dolls (1955), on the other hand, was an instant success. Not actually an M-G-M product, it was made by the Samuel Goldwyn Company and distributed by Metro-Goldwyn-Mayer.

Based on the Broadway hit by Frank Loesser, *Guys and Dolls* starred Marlon Brando as Sky Masterson, Jean Simmons as Sarah Brown, Frank Sinatra as Nathan Detroit and Vivian Blaine as Miss Adelaide, a selection of Damon Runyon's characters, and the script by the director Joseph L Mankiewicz was based on the Runyon story, 'The Idyll of Sarah

Holden, Walter Pidgeon and, as the only female board member, Barbara Stanwyck, in a believable study of office maneuverings.

One of the fastest films ever made was *The Blackboard Jungle* (1955) a frightening indictment of big city schools. Richard Brooks directed his own script, based on Evan Hunter's powerful novel, with such speed that the film was ready for release in three months.

The cast headed by Glenn Ford as the idealistic, but aware teacher, was excellent, and included Anne Francis, Sidney Poitier, Vic Morrow and Louis Calhern, who shouldn't have had time to breathe in the fifties. One of the big selling points of the film was the inclusion on the score of Bill Haley and the Comets' recording of 'Rock Around the Clock.'

Opposite top: *William Holden, Dean Jagger, Louis Calhern and Fredric March in Executive Suite (1954).*
Opposite below: *Sidney Poitier (right) and Glenn Ford – The Blackboard Jungle (1955).*

Right: *During 'The Oldest Established Permanent Floating Crap Game In New York,' Marlon Brando sings 'Luck Be A Lady Tonight' with Frank Sinatra (right rear) in Guys and Dolls (1955).*
Below right: *Lalume (Dolores Grey) and Hajj (Howard Keel) in Kismet (1955).*
Below: *It's Always Fair Weather (1955), with Michael Kidd, Gene Kelly and Dan Dailey.*

Brown.' Several of the other characters like Nicely-Nicely Johnson, Benny Southstreet and the other gamblers also appeared. The ladies and Sinatra acquitted themselves well, but Brando was miscast as Sky Masterson.

The score retained many of the Broadway show-stopping numbers including Sky Masterson's 'Luck Be A Lady Tonight,' Sarah's lovely 'If I Were a Bell' and Adelaide's strip 'Take Back Your Mink.' The film opened with the wonderful 'Fugue for Tinhorns,' ('I've Got The Horse Right Here') and had Michael Kidd's choreography to enliven 'The Oldest Established Permanent Floating Crap Game in New York.'

Another Broadway musical came to the screen in 1955. This was *Kismet*, based on the Edward Knoblock play which opened in 1912 with Otis Skinner. Skinner made two film versions of the play, a silent one in 1920, and an early sound edition ten years later. In 1944, it was remade starring Ronald Colman as the beggar-poet Hajj and Marlene Dietrich as the lovely Lalume.

Robert Wright and George Forrest had created a memorable score, based on the music of Alexander Borodin, for the stage play and it was this version that M-G-M made with Howard Keel as Hajj, Dolores Gray as Lalume, Ann Blyth as Hajj's daughter Marsinah and Vic Damone as the caliph, who disguises himself, in the manner beloved of all storybook caliphs, and falls in love with the beggar-poet's daughter.

The score included 'And This Is My Beloved,' 'Baubles, Bangles and Beads' and the lovely 'Stranger in Paradise.' Vincente Minnelli directed and Arthur Freed was the producer of this lavish musical based on the Arabian Nights tales.

In 1955 M-G-M made a series of biographies about singers who had to overcome a disability. *Interrupted Melody* (1955) was the story of opera soprano Marjorie Lawrence's battle with polio, starring Eleanor Parker, with voice dubbed by Eileen Farrell. *Love Me Or Leave Me* (1955) starred Doris Day as Ruth Etting, whose problem was her husband, a racketeer, played by James Cagney. Day did her own singing, as did Susan Hayward in *I'll Cry Tomorrow* (1955) as film star Lillian Roth, whose career was curtailed by acute alcoholism.

The script was by Helen Deutsch, who adapted Miss Roth's autobiography. The director was Daniel Mann and Hayward's costars included Richard Conte, Eddie Albert and Jo Van Fleet.

With a lovely sense of timing, M-G-M managed to release *The Swan* (1956) just before the star, Grace Kelly, became Her Serene Highness, the Princess of Monaco. An adaptation of Ferenc Molnár's play, *The Swan* was the story of a princess whose kingdom had disappeared in the reshuffle of Europe after the Napoleonic Wars. She has, however, been trained to marry a monarch, and while being courted by a king, Alec Guinness, finds herself falling in love with her brother's tutor, Louis Jourdan. The young man is dismissed, but before that she is made to realize their romance would have led nowhere. She has been subtly changed for the good, and the king, who accepts her, is worldly enough to realize this will make her a better queen.

As usual, the production by Cedric Gibbons was meticulous in conjuring up the life of a small court in exile, and Agnes Moorehead, Estelle Winwood and Jessie Royce Landis

were superb as the ladies of the court, her mother and aunts.

Grace Kelly's last part for M-G-M completed just before her departure for Monaco was as Tracy Lord in *High Society* (1956), a musical based on *The Philadelphia Story*. As in the original, Tracy is an icy well-bred young divorcée whose second marriage to John Lund is interrupted by the appearance of her ex-husband Bing Crosby. The reporters Mike Connor and Liz Imbrie were now played by Frank Sinatra and Celeste Holm.

The setting of the film had been changed to Newport, Rhode Island, to take advantage of the jazz festival and give a reason for including jazz great Louis Armstrong and his band in the proceedings.

The songs by Cole Porter included 'True Love,' which Crosby and Kelly sang together; 'I Love You Samantha;' 'Mind If I Make Love To You,' which Sinatra sang to Grace Kelly; the humorous 'Who Wants To Be A Millionaire' ('I Don't'), which Sinatra sang with Celeste Holm and 'Well, Did You Evah,' which he sang with Crosby. That song had been written by Porter for *DuBarry Was a Lady* in 1939, where it was sung on Broadway by Betty Grable and Charles Walters. It was Walters who directed *High Society* and was probably responsible for the song's inclusion.

Louis Armstrong and his band were featured in the opening 'High Society Calypso' and he had a wonderful duet with Crosby, which gave a little solo to each member of his band,

Opposite top: *The beggar-poet Hajj (Howard Keel) and his daughter Marsinah (Ann Blyth) on the streets of Bagdad in* Kismet *(1955).*

Opposite far left: *Susan Hayward (left) as Lillian Roth in* I'll Cry Tomorrow *(1955), here with Margo.*

Opposite left: *Grace Kelly tries to persuade Louis Jourdan to not leave his position as tutor to her brothers in* The Swan *(1956).*

Right: *Tracy Lord (Grace Kelly) appears after a midnight swim with Mike Connor (Frank Sinatra). Her ex-husband C K Dexter-Haven (Bing Crosby) doesn't seem to mind.* High Society *(1956).*

'Now You Has Jazz.' The film marked the final screen performance of Louis Calhern, who played Uncle Willie.

It was a tremendous success, not altogether because of the star's wedding. Crosby may have been a trifle old for the part, but he never sounded better, nor did Sinatra.

Kirk Douglas and Anthony Quinn costarred as the painters Vincent van Gogh and Paul Gauguin in *Lust for Life* (1956), an adaptation of Irving Stone's novel of Van Gogh's life and pathetic death. James Donald played van Gogh's brother Theo, who also narrates the story of a man's descent into madness.

The exteriors were shot on location in France and Holland, giving the audience an opportunity to compare the landscapes with the paintings Douglas seemed to be creating. Vincente Minnelli directed and Cedric Gibbons once again did the art direction, and was nominated for an Academy Award. Anthony Quinn won the Oscar as Best Supporting Actor for his overpowering performance as Gauguin.

M-G-M took another stab at Shakespeare when Irving Block and Allan Adler borrowed the plot of *The Tempest* for a science-fiction film called *Forbidden Planet* (1956). The island of Prospero has been translated to the planet of Altair IV, where Dr Morbius (Walter Pidgeon) and his daughter (Anne Francis) are the only survivors of a space colony. When a space mission led by Commander Adams (Leslie Nielsen) arrives on the planet, they discover that the destruction of the colony was caused by the thought patterns of the inhabitants which were transformed into a destructive force by machinery created by an extinct race. By suppressing his demon, Dr Morbius permits his daughter and the members of the mission to escape before he allows the planet to be destroyed.

The comic relief and Ariel of this film was Robbie the Robot, the first in a long line of androids smarter and more amusing than those who programed them. The director was Cyril Fred McLeod Wilcox and the script was by Cyril Hume.

Somebody Up There Likes Me (1956) was the biography of boxing great Rocky Graziano, starring Paul Newman. The film followed his career from the slums through a prison sentence to the middleweight championship. Pier Angeli costarred as Rocky's girlfriend, and the cast also included Everett Sloane, Eileen Heckert and Sal Mineo.

The stark screenplay was written by Ernest Lehman and based on Graziano's autobiography. Robert Wise directed, and the art department, headed by Cedric Gibbons, did their usual deft job and were awarded the Oscar for best art direction for a black and white film. The cinematography by Joseph Ruttenberg was also given an award.

In *The Teahouse Of The August Moon* (1956), Marlon Brando played an Okinawan translator named Sakini, who was employed by Glenn Ford, a captain in the US Army of Occupation. Based on the novel by Vern J Sneider and the

Right: *Dr Morbius (Walter Pidgeon) and his daughter (Anne Francis) welcome Commander Adams (Leslie Nielsen) to the* Forbidden Planet *(1956). Robbie the Robot is on the left.*
Opposite: *Vincent van Gogh (Kirk Douglas) tries to explain his art to his brother Theo (James Donald) in* Lust for Life *(1956).*

Below: *The victorious fighter Rocky Graziano (Paul Newman) is driven through the streets of New York, with his girl (Pier Angeli) in* Somebody Up There Likes Me *(1956).*

play by John Patrick, the plot concerned a village on Okinawa just after the war, and how the lives of the inhabitants are changed by the occupying army and vice-versa.

Eddie Albert costarred as an army psychiatrist who goes overboard in trying to understand the Okinawan ways, and the cast also included Machiko Kyo and Nijikyo Kiyokawa as the two geishas given to the commanding officer in an early incident of cultural confusion. Paul Ford (who took over for Louis Calhern after that great actor's untimely death) was Colonel Purdy, the commanding officer, the role he had played on Broadway.

The director was Delbert Mann and the picture was shot on location in Japan. The art directors were William Horning and Eddie Imazu, who designed a charming Okinawan village down to the last pavilion for the tea ceremony in the garden of the commanding officer's quarters.

M-G-M tried to repeat the success of *Gone With The Wind* with their adaptation of another long novel with a Civil War setting. This was Ross Lockridge's *Raintree County* (1957), which became a sprawling, expensive ($6,000,000) epic starring Elizabeth Taylor and Montgomery Clift.

Despite good performances by Taylor as the southern belle whose high spirits contain the seeds of her tragic disintegration and insanity, and Clift as the man she tricked into marrying her, the film was too vague to hold the audience's attention. Perhaps in the hopes of detracting from the flaws in the script by Millard Kaufman, the production was as lavish and detailed as M-G-M could make it.

Taylor received her first Academy Award nomination as Susanna Drake. Nominations also went to Walter Plunkett for costume design and William A Horning and Urie McLeary, who were responsible for the art decoration.

One of the most popular and profitable M-G-M films of the year was *Jailhouse Rock* (1957) which brought in $4,000,000, thanks to the presence of a new star, rock singer Elvis Presley. The plot, which cast Presley as a young convict serving a term for manslaughter who learns to play the guitar and become a popular singer, was less important to the audience than the sound track, which featured their idol in several songs, including 'I Want To Be Free,' 'Baby, I Don't Care' and the raucous title song.

Not a remake, but a film which looked at *The Story of Emile Zola* (Warner Bros., 1937) from a different angle, was *I Accuse* (1957), starring Jose Ferrer as the Jewish French Army Captain Dreyfus accused of treason. The script by Gore Vidal concentrated on Dreyfus, following him through the trial and imprisonment at Devil's Island to exoneration when the plot to discredit him is uncovered with the aid of Zola, among others. Ferrer also directed, and his costars included Viveca Lindfors as his wife, and Anton Walbrook, Leo Genn, Emlyn Williams and Donald Wolfit. Since the film was shot at the British studio, producer Sam Zimbalist was able to take advantage of the British actors currently at work in London's West End.

Above: *Montgomery Clift and Elizabeth Taylor starred in* Raintree County *(1957).*
Right: *Elvis Presley as the young convict in* Jailhouse Rock *(1957).*

Opposite: *A village celebration in* The Teahouse Of The August Moon *(1956) with Marlon Brando, Glenn Ford and Eddie Albert.*

A more ambitious effort was Pandro S Berman's production of *The Brothers Karamazov* (1957). This was a handsomely mounted adaptation of Dostoyevsky's novel which starred Yul Brynner and Maria Schell. The direction by Richard Brooks, who also wrote the screenplay, tried to cover too much of the very philosophical novel which told the story of family rivalry in pre-revolutionary Russia. Costar Lee J Cobb received an Academy Award nomination for his supporting role as the dominating father.

Nineteen-fifty-eight was, for M-G-M, the year of *Gigi*, their award-winning musical adaptation of the play by Colette about a young girl in a family of demi-mondaines who manages to marry the man her family has set up to be her protector. The screenplay by Alan Jay Lerner captured all the naughtiness of *fin de siecle* Paris, which was also brilliantly captured by the costumes and art direction.

Leslie Caron had the best part of her career as Gigi, the girl who is young enough to ride a donkey on the sands in one scene and old enough to be transformed by a few very fine feathers designed by Cecil Beaton into a heartbreakingly lovely woman. Her costars included Louis Jourdan as Gaston Lachaille, the young aristocrat who suddenly finds himself in love with his young friend, and Maurice Chevalier, who returned to M-G-M to play Honoré, Gaston's uncle who once

had an affair with Mme Alvarez, Gigi's aunt (played with humor and a slight touch of wickedness by Hermione Gingold).

The score by Lerner and Frederick Loewe began on a high note, with Chevalier singing 'Thank Heaven for Little Girls,' went on to a duet with Jourdan in which the younger man explained how life had lost its zest, 'It's a Bore.' Other highlights were the joyful, 'The Night They Invented Champagne,' in which Gigi wins her first taste of the drink by cheating in her usual card game with Gaston, and 'I Remember It Well,' a scene when Honoré and Mme Alvarez compare their joint memories. Finally, there is the finale, in which Gaston realizes that it is Gigi he loves. This involved wonderful shots of Paris by night as Gaston walks through the city trying to understand his own mind.

Most of *Gigi*'s exteriors were shot in Paris, as were the two scenes at Maxim's, the renowned French restaurant that agreed to close for three days to allow filming. The chief cameraman, Joe Ruttenberg, had a technical difficulty with the famous mirrors that cover the restaurant's walls, and managed to light the set, without having the huge studio lamps reflected in every shot, by attaching them to the ceiling with suction cups.

Once again, the producer Arthur Freed and the director

Vincente Minnelli had a winner, and it was their biggest box office success. It also earned nine Oscars, including Best Picture and Best Direction, as well as Best Song, 'Gigi,' and the art direction, cinematography, costume and film editing awards. The last two Oscars went to Alan Lerner for his screenplay and to Lerner and Loewe for the score.

M-G-M had another spectacular success with *Cat On A Hot Tin Roof* (1958) which not only made more money than *Gigi*, but became one of their ten biggest moneymakers all told. An adaptation of Tennessee William's play, the film starred Paul Newman as Brick, and Elizabeth Taylor as his wife, Maggie, a role the studio had scheduled for Grace Kelly.

Cat takes place on the Mississippi plantation of Big Daddy Pollitt (Burl Ives) where the family has gathered to celebrate his 65th birthday. Big Daddy is not aware that he is dying of cancer, as his older son Gooper, (Jack Carson) and his wife Mae (Madeleine Sherwood) and Big Mama (Judith Anderson) are concealing it. Brick and Maggie are also there for the festivities, but Brick is keeping to their room, having broken his ankle, is drinking heavily and avoiding the advances of his wife since he believes her to have been unfaithful to him with Skipper, the college friend he idolized, who has committed suicide.

Maggie is trying to get Brick to sleep with her partly because she loves him, but also because a child would negate

Top right: *Leslie Caron as the schoolgirl who becomes a glamorous woman in* Gigi *(1958).*
Opposite: The Brothers Karamazov *(1957) starred Yul Brynner and Maria Schell.*

Right: *Maurice Chevalier as the worldly boulevardier Honoré Lachaille, sings 'Thank Heaven For Little Girls' in* Gigi *(1958).*

the threat of Gooper's 'little no-necked monsters' inheriting Brick's share of Big Daddy's estate. Brick's friendship with Skipper is implied to have been more than that, and the double betrayal by wife and best friend has sent him to the bottle, as well as his feeling of guilt for not responding to a phone call from Skipper before he died. Big Daddy confronts him with this, and to retaliate Brick tells him he has cancer.

The catharsis of admitting guilt, plus Maggie's loyalty, brings Brick out of his self-imposed exile and he prepares to make true Maggie's lie that she is pregnant.

The deletions of any overt references to homosexuality which were found in the play were caused primarily by the Production Code. Director Richard Brooks managed to get the spirit of the original play into the film, but many of the reviews criticized him precisely on this point, that he had eliminated the thread of homosexuality, when they should have been aware that the Production Code would never have passed the script otherwise.

Newman's performance was one of his best, and Taylor was brilliant as Maggie, one of her first serious roles. She was nominated for Best Actress for it, and Newman for Best Actor. The real surprise to many moviegoers was folk-singer Burl Ives, who was repeating the role of Big Daddy after its Broadway success.

Spectacular films were quite common in the late fifties. All the studios made them, although few were as large as the 1959 edition of *Ben Hur*. This time, it was M-G-M who was in financial trouble when they began the film, feeling that an epic, which was bound to bring in tremendous receipts, might maintain their tenuous profit margin. To cut down on costs, the film was made at the vast studio outside Rome, Cinecittá, where *Quo Vadis* was filmed in 1951.

Karl Tunberg went back to the original novel, rather than basing his script on the play as Carey Wilson and Bess Meredyth had in 1925. This gave him the opportunity to eliminate some extraneous material and anachronisms that had crept into the original film. He had help in this from the British poet and playwright, Christopher Fry. The director was William Wyler.

After some hesitation Charlton Heston was cast as the title character, although several other actors had been considered for the role, including Burt Lancaster, Rock Hudson and Cesare Danova. In fact, Heston had once been considered for the part of Messala, which was given to Stephen Boyd. An Israeli actress, Haya Harareet, was cast as Esther, Sam Jaffe as Simonides, the faithful steward, Martha Scott as Ben Hur's mother, Miriam, and Cathy O'Donnell as his sister Tirzah. Other parts were played by Jack Hawkins as Arrius, Hugh Griffith as Sheik Ilderim and Finlay Currie as the Wise Man.

Despite the author's subtitle 'A Story of the Christ' and the presence of Esther, *Ben Hur* is really a story of the two men, Ben Hur, the Jew, and Messala, the Roman, and their friendship which turns to hatred. Messala cannot understand that his boyhood friend would actually side with his own people rather than the governing Romans. When Ben Hur is arrested after a tile falls off the roof of his house and startles the new governor's horse, Messala decides to make an example of his old friend and sentences him to the galleys. It is Messala's vindictiveness in imprisoning Ben Hur's mother and sister which really seals his hatred for the Roman. The feelings of

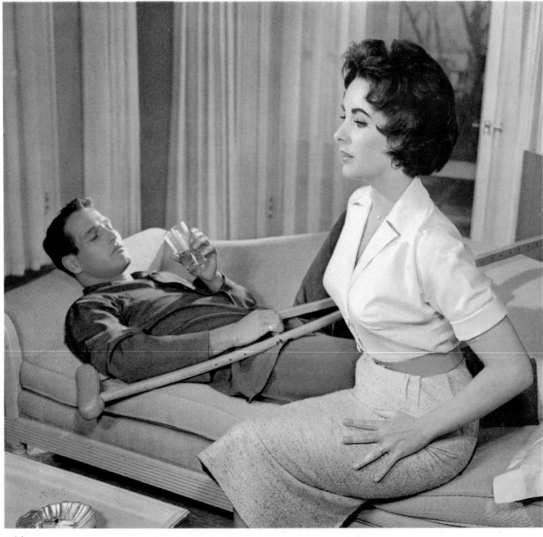

Right: *Leonard (Martin Landau) forces a drink on Roger Thornhill (Cary Grant) who is being held against his will and by mistake in* North by Northwest *(1959).*

Opposite: *Paul Newman as Brick and Elizabeth Taylor as Maggie in* Cat On A Hot Tin Roof *(1958).*
Below: *Ben Hur's chariot jumps over one of the crashed competitors. The driver is actually the stuntman Joe Canutt –* Ben Hur *(1959).*

forgiveness Ben Hur experiences seeing Messala mutilated and dying after the chariot race are immediately washed away upon hearing that his mother and sister are alive, but lepers, after their imprisonment. Once Messala is dead, the conflict is resolved and the rest of the film, which includes the Crucifixion, is somewhat of an anti-climax. This feeling may also arise because the great action episode of the film, the chariot race, is also over.

Of the two great action scenes in the film, the chariot race is the more exciting. The battle at sea in the galleys was done in a tank with miniatures, and is missing the sense of reality that is present at the race. Once again, M-G-M built a vast arena, which was over five stories in height, and the stands held some 8000 extras. Seventy-eight horses were trained for the race, although only eight teams raced. The second unit director who was in charge of the race was Yakima Canutt, who also designed the special (if inaccurate) two-rein harness worn by the horses. He also trained many of the drivers, including Heston, who did all his own stunt work except for a jump over the wreckage of two chariots. The driver in the long shot is Yakima Canutt's son, Joe. Wyler, the director, also shot closeups the day of the race which were intercut with Canutt's long shots and gave the race its sense of personal competition between Messala and Ben Hur.

At the Academy Awards, *Ben Hur* won a record 12 Oscars including Best Picture, Best Actor (Heston), Best Supporting Actor (Hugh Griffith), Best Director and many technical and special effects awards. The score by Miklos Rosza was also honored. Despite its length, for it ran for 217 minutes and had an intermission, the film was a phenomenal success. Once again *Ben Hur* had rescued M-G-M.

North by Northwest was the only M-G-M film made by the veteran director Alfred Hitchcock, and it is considered one of

his best. It is a thriller along the lines of *The Man Who Knew Too Much* (GB, 1934) or *The Thirty-Nine Steps* (GB, 1935), rather than one of the horror pictures for which he is somewhat better known.

Once again, the Hitchcock hero becomes involved unexpectedly with secret agents. Kidnapped by mistake by a spy ring, Roger Thornhill cannot convince them of his innocence. They force him to become drunk, planning him to have an automobile accident on the way home. Instead he is picked up by the police, who do not believe his story. He tracks down the real owner of the house where he was held, only to have the man fall dead in his arms from a knife in the back before his innocence can be established. To prove he is not guilty he heads for Chicago on the Twentieth Century Limited, on which he meets Eve Kendall, who hides him in her compartment while the police search the train. From Chicago she sends him to a mysterious meeting in Indiana where he is almost killed by a crop-dusting plane. He manages to get back to Chicago and confronts Eve. Later he tracks her to an auction house where she is seated with Vandamm, the head of the spy ring. When trapped there by two of the spy ring, the hero makes a scene, forcing his arrest by the police. They release him into the custody of the Professor, a government agent, who explains that Eve is a government agent as well, and in danger. The hero agrees to help rescue her. This takes him to South Dakota, and a scramble across

the presidential profiles on Mount Rushmore. The head of the spy ring falls off the mountain, and Eve and the hero are saved.

Cary Grant played Roger Thornhill, and gave a great performance as the archetypal Hitchcock hero, in a slightly tongue-in-cheek manner which may have given the audience the idea that he was never truly in danger. Eve Kendall was played by Eva Marie Saint, one of Hitchcock's icy blondes, not unlike Kim Novak or Grace Kelly. Others in the cast included James Mason as Vandamm, Leo G Carroll as the Professor, both of whom turned in their usual sterling performance.

Hitchcock had been scheduled to direct *The Wreck of the Mary Deare* (1959), but decided to make *North by Northwest* instead. So the direction chores for Eric Ambler's adaptation of the Hammond Innes' novel were given to Michael Anderson.

The stars were Gary Cooper and Charlton Heston in a thriller adventure about a shipwreck which is part of an insurance scheme. The photography by Joseph Ruttenberg was very well done, being full of mist, fog and a truly frightening underwater sequence as the two heroes try to obtain the evidence that will clear Cooper's name and reveal the conspiracy to defraud.

Once again, the Arthur Freed unit produced a sterling film adaptation of a Broadway hit, with *Bells Are Ringing* (1960). Starring Judy Holliday, who was repeating her Broadway success, *Bells Are Ringing* was the story of a telephone answering service run by Jean Stapleton, who was also reprising her Broadway role, with the aid of Holliday. Among her clients are a playwright (Dean Martin) with writer's block and Eddie Foy, as the bookmaker who annexes the answering service for his office.

The book was by Betty Comden and Adolph Green, who had worked at M-G-M on many of the musicals for the Freed unit, and the music was by Jule Styne. The score included a number of songs that have now become standards, including 'The Party's Over,' 'Just In Time' and 'Long Before I Knew You.'

Unfortunately the public's taste had changed and the film did not do well. The Freed musical unit was dispersed as part of the economic cuts instigated by the changing administrations who had taken over the running of the studio, following the ouster of Mayer in 1951.

The studio had been behind hand in accepting the successful invasion of television and the independent production units which arose as the big studios fell into decline. They had also neglected to arrange to distribute the productions of these independents, which would have given them some revenue and films in the Loew's Inc theaters.

The changes in policy instigated in the studio by Dore Schary were not all appreciated. A good number of the executives were still Mayer's men, and office politics led to disagreements between the studio in California and Loew's Inc in New York, even before the resignation of Nick Schenk, who had been the president of Loew's since the very beginning.

The new president, Arthur Loew, a son of the founder, lasted for less than a year in the position, although during that time he instigated one policy that would guarantee continuing revenue to the company. He decided to lease the valuable back-log of M-G-M films to television rather than selling them outright, which most of the other studios had done.

Schary and Loew both resigned a year later, blamed by the stockholders, in the usual way, for low investment returns in light of high studio expenses.

After Loew's resignation, Louis B Mayer made an attempt to take over the company with the aid of a television producer Stanley Meyer and a Canadian financier named Tomlinson, who owned the largest block of Loew's stock. Before the stockholders meeting, Mayer backed out, partly because he realized that he would have to deal with the business side of movie-making rather than the creative, and he didn't have the physical strength to complete the deal. He died of leukemia two months later in October 1957.

Another major change came in 1959, when M-G-M was finally divided from the theater-owning company of Loew's, the last of the studios to accept the government's anti-trust action.

Under the continuous pressure of big business, the industry had changed. This was a new Hollywood.

Opposite: *Charlton Heston and Gary Cooper* – The Wreck of the Mary Deare *(1959).*

Below: *Dean Martin, Judy Holliday (left) and Fred Clark* – Bells Are Ringing *(1960).*

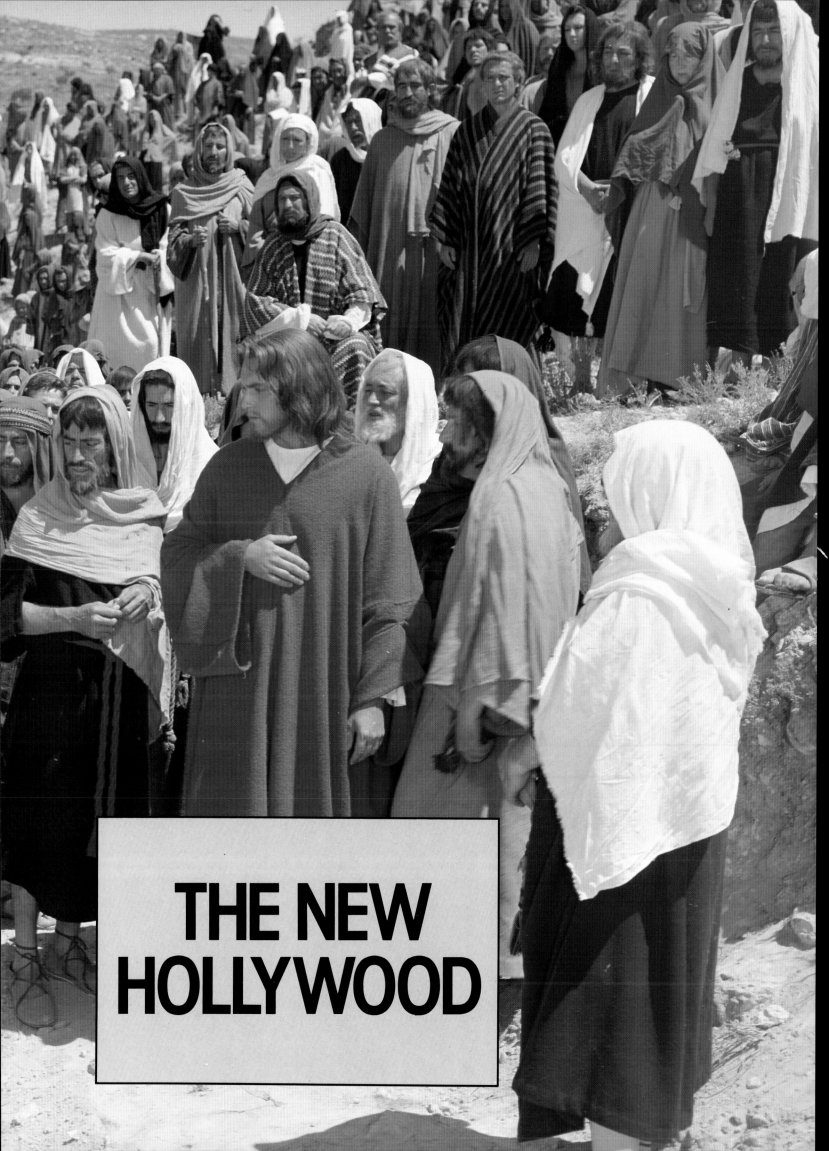

THE NEW HOLLYWOOD

THE DIVESTMENT OF THE theaters made no great difference in M-G-M profits, but expenses in Hollywood were still high. The wonderful labor pool that the great studios had created was rife with featherbedding, but the major studios were not producing many movies and the smaller studios could not afford to pay these individuals their worth.

Audience taste continued to shift, and to cope with it M-G-M made distribution deals with a number of overseas companies for movies like *The Giant Of Marathon* or *The Colossus of Rhodes* which were both well received, especially at the drive-ins. The same audience was considered when M-G-M made *Where The Boys Are* (1960) and *Platinum High School* (1960).

The studio was still producing movies for a more adult audience. In the case of *Butterfield 8* (1960), a very adult audience indeed. The title derived from the telephone exchange of Gloria Wandrous, a model who is also a call girl. Gloria (Elizabeth Taylor) is used to having her own way with men, and when the married man she does fall in love with seems hesitant about leaving his wife, she kills herself in an automobile accident.

Laurence Harvey co-starred as the married lover and Dina Merrill played his wife. Eddie Fisher played Gloria's only male friend and Susan Oliver was very good as his jealous girl friend.

The film was adapted from John O'Hara's novel, which was

Right: *George Sanders with the mysterious children, including Martin Stephens (left) as his son in* Village of the Damned *(1960).*
Previous spread: *Christ (Jeffrey Hunter) preaching to the multitudes in* King of Kings *(1961)*

Opposite: *Elizabeth Taylor won an Academy Award as Best Actress in 1960 for her performance in* Butterfield 8 *(1960).*
Below right: *Rod Taylor returns to his study in the future in* The Time Machine *(1960).*

based on a real incident concerning Starr Faithful, a New York socialite who died under mysterious circumstances in the 1920s. The director was Daniel Mann and Pandro S Berman produced the film which was the biggest M-G-M moneymaker for that year.

Another great success was *The Time Machine* (1960), based on the novel by H G Wells. The plot concerned a young scientist (Rod Taylor) who invents a machine (all wood, brass fittings and plush) which will transport him through time. After witnessing an atomic conflict he pushes the machine further into the future, arriving at a time when mankind had divided into two distinct groups. One, the Eloi, are peaceful, gentle blonde beings. The others, the Morlocks, are brutal cave dwellers who use the ancient air raid sirens to summon the Eloi into caves and butcher them for food. The young scientist falls in love with one of the Eloi (Yvette Mimieux) and inspires the others to defend themselves against the Morlocks.

The producer and director, George Pal, was renowned for special effects, his previous films included *The War of the Worlds* (1951), and *When Worlds Collide* (1953) and he created some wonderful ones for *The Time Machine*, especially the catastrophic atomic war, and the passage of time, which is indicated by the changing fashions on a window mannequin in a show outside the scientist's laboratory. The screenplay, by David Duncan, emphasized the fear of atomic war that was a way of life at that time, and also showed a form of survival.

Another view of the future was seen in *The Village of the Damned* (1960). The screenplay, by Sterling Silliphant, George Barclay and director Wolf Rilla, was an adaptation of John Wyndham's novel *The Midwich Cuckoos*, which told of a village in which all the women capable of fertility become pregnant at the same time. The children, when delivered, are preternaturally intelligent and utterly emotionless. As they grow, they begin a studied pattern of taking over the minds of

those they distrust and destroying them. Eventually, one of the fathers (George Sanders, in an unusually sympathetic role) manages to hold his mind against them until a bomb planted in his briefcase explodes, destroying them all.

Rilla created a number of wonderful images in the films, focusing in the beginning on the emotions of the women who become pregnant, which range from delight on the part of a previously childless wife, to despair for young girls and the wife of a sailor who has been at sea for half a year. He also created a believable bond between the children, who are treated as outsiders by the rest of the villagers, who are alternately afraid and ashamed of them. And there is a wonderfully frightening scene where one of the children, about a year old, wills his mother to scald herself in punishment for ignoring him. It was one of the best films to come out of the British M-G-M studio, and marked the debut of Martin Stephens as one of the children.

Nineteen sixty-one marked the year of the largest M-G-M profits to date, but that was due to *Ben Hur* and a re-release of *Gone With The Wind*. The film which was expected to be the big hit of the year was *King of Kings* (1961). The story of Christ was retold, with Jeffrey Hunter in the title role. A better actor may have salvaged something of the film, which became rudely known as 'I Was A Teenage Jesus.' Hunter's performance might have been better if his dialogue hadn't needed re-recording.

Good performances by Siobhan McKenna as the Virgin, Robert Ryan as John the Baptist, and Hurd Hatfield as Pontius Pilate couldn't save the film, and the critics hated it. The public, however, was less unkind, and certainly enjoyed the spectacular aspects of the movie, which had overpowered the spiritual.

Right: *James Mason as Humbert Humbert and Sue Lyon as the nymphet,* Lolita *(1962).*

Opposite top: *The Sermon on the Mount from* King of Kings *(1961).*
Opposite below: *Gregory Peck, Thelma Ritter, Robert Preston and Debbie Reynolds on the wagon train in* How The West Was Won *(1962).*

The big picture of 1962 was *How The West Was Won,* the first film shot in Cinerama to have a plot. Cinerama, a wide screen process that used three cameras to shoot, and three projectors to view, had been around since the early fifties, but its novelty had worn off. The story of the American westward movement seemed about the right size to fill its screen, and engender new interest.

The film followed one family from the east, onto a flatboat on the Ohio and to an early settlement there. One daughter (Carroll Baker) marries a fur trapper (James Stewart); the other, Debbie Reynolds, joins a wagon train crossing the plains and meets a gambler (Gregory Peck). The Civil War intervenes, and afterwards, the son of Baker and Stewart joins the cavalry to deal with the Indians, and later becomes a marshal to deal with outlaws.

The film used three veteran directors, which also allowed three aspects of the film to be made at the same time. Henry Hathaway handled 'The Rivers' and 'The Plains,' George Marshall 'The Outlaws' and John Ford 'The Civil War,' which featured a nice scene with John Wayne as Sherman and Harry Morgan as Grant.

Other parts were played by Robert Preston as the wagon train master, Richard Widmark as the head of a railroad gang, Raymond Massey as Abraham Lincoln and Eli Wallach as the head of the outlaw gang. A narration by Spencer Tracy linked the episodes together.

The plot allowed for plenty of action, which was heightened by the Cinerama process. The flatboat trip finishes with a crash and sinking after voyaging through rapids. The wagon train is attacked by Indians. A buffalo stampede interrupts the laying of the railroad (and in the film's most memorable

scene, knocks over a water tower). The pursuit of the outlaws involves a fight on a train crossing a trestle. All the standard elements of the great Westerns were used.

The film played well in Cinerama houses, and in theaters where the film was shown on a flat screen, although the occasional seams where the three films had been joined could be seen.

One of the most surprising hits of 1962 was *Lolita,* based on the novel of Vladimir Nabokov. The novel had raised some eyebrows with its description of an older man's obsession with a very young girl, and was deemed unfilmable. Nabokov himself wrote the screenplay, cleverly opening with the ending, and raising the age of the girl to a teenager, as well as avoiding any possible sensationalism.

James Mason played Humbert Humbert, that man who marries the nouveau-riche widow in order to court her young daughter. Shelley Winters was well cast as the pretentious mother, but Sue Lyon was too awkward in her role as the flirtatious Lolita. Peter Sellers played Clare Quilty, the psychiatrist. The director was Stanley Kubrick.

Four years after *Cat On A Hot Tin Roof,* Paul Newman appeared in another Tennessee Williams film, *Sweet Bird Of Youth* (1962). Again the director was Richard Brooks, who also wrote the screenplay.

Newman, repeating his Broadway success, played Chance Wayne, an aspiring actor, who is being kept by the fading star, Alexandra del Lago (Geraldine Page, also repeating a Broadway triumph). She is sure that her latest picture will be a failure, and with Chance is roaming about the United States to avoid contact with anybody she knows. They return to the town Chance grew up in and left hurriedly after an affair with

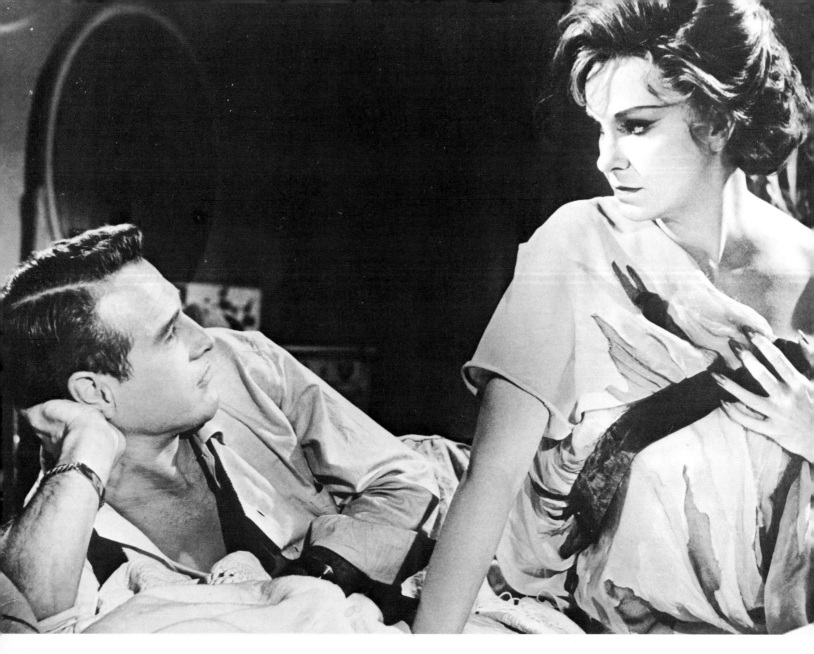

Heavenly, the daughter of Boss Finley, the local corrupt politician, resulted in her pregnancy.

Despite his duties to Alexandra, whom he sees as his ticket to Hollywood, Chance seizes a moment to meet the girl, although her brother and father have sworn to destroy him. Alexandra learns that her film was a success, and she leaves Chance to face the Finleys alone. He is beaten up, but leaves town with the girl anyway.

The ending of the play was radically changed by Brooks to deal with the strictures of the Production Code, which still had to be placated. The semi-happy ending was also due to the Hollywood belief that that was what the public wanted.

Despite this, the reviews for the cast were uniformly good, and Newman and Page especially were cited for their performances. Brooks' changes once again were castigated by the reviewers.

M-G-M had not been well-known for Westerns, but in 1962 they brought out one of the finest, *Ride the High Country*. Set at the end of the last century when the old west was to all intents and purposes finished, *Ride the High Country* tells of two old lawmen, who are given one more chance to prove themselves as civilization encroaches on the world they once knew. Steve Judd (Joel McCrea) takes a job escorting a gold shipment from a remote mining town, and hires his old deputy Gil Westrum (Randolph Scott) to help him. With Westrum comes a young friend Heck Longtree (Ronald Starr).

On their way to the mining town, they spend the night at the Knudsen cabin. The daughter, Elsa (Mariette Hartley) has accepted a proposal from Billy Hammond to escape her stern father, and the three offer to escort her to the mining town for her wedding. On their arrival they discover that her fiancée and his family live in squalor, and she would be treated as common property by the entire family.

She joins them on their trip back with the gold, although they are being followed by the Hammonds, who want Elsa and the gold as well. Westrum takes the gold, a plan that had been in his mind from the beginning, leaving the other three to face the Hammonds at the Knudsen cabin, where the Hammonds have murdered Elsa's father. Young Heck is wounded, and Judd is holding off the Hammonds single-handedly when Westrum returns, having had a change of heart. Together he and Judd challenge the three Hammonds and kill them, but Judd is badly wounded. He sends Westrum, Elsa and Heck back with the gold, knowing it will be delivered, and dies content.

The presence of the two veteran cowboy actors, McCrea and Scott, gives the film a sense of reality which is increased by Sam Peckinpah's direction, which allows the West to be a grubby, sordid place, once man tries to tame it. The genuinely sympathetic characters give the audience a rallying point, and the villains are equally repellent, emphasizing the director's feeling for an era that is finished.

The photography by Lucien Ballard also help distinguish

between the beauty of what was past, and the impatient mechanized future. The film was the last for both McCrea and Scott, who retired after movie careers that began in the late twenties.

In 1960 M-G-M began pre-production on a remake of one of their great hits of the 1930s, *Mutiny On The Bounty*, which finally was released at the end of 1962. When the project was started, producer Aaron Rosenberg planned a duplicate of the 1935 hit with Charles Laughton and Clark Gable, but he wanted Marlon Brando to play Fletcher Christian. Brando was not interested unless the screenplay were changed to emphasize the mutineers and their struggle.

Delays in the script and the building of the *Bounty* replica led to the resignation of writer Eric Ambler and the director

Sir Carol Reed. Reed was replaced by Lewis Milestone, who did not get on with his star, and Ambler by Charles Lederer.

The finished film may have been closer to the historical mutiny, for many of the fictional elements, including the character of the narrator, Midshipman Byam, had been eliminated. Brando, for reasons known only to himself, chose to play the Manx Master's Mate as a court fop, though after the mutiny his characterization became more believable. Trevor Howard, as Captain Bligh was less given to overblown villainy than Laughton had been. Visually however, the film was flawless, filled with wonderful shots of the Bounty under sail, in the storm as she doubles Cape Horn and the cheerful native welcome to Tahiti.

The most recent version of the Bounty tale was made in 1980, by Orion Pictures, an independent company, and

Opposite: *Chance Wayne (Paul Newman) and Alexandra del Lago (Geraldine Page) in* Sweet Bird Of Youth *(1962).*

Right: *Joel McCrea, Mariette Hartley and Ronald Starr starred in* Ride the High Country *(1962).*
Below: *Fletcher Christian (Marlon Brando) takes command of the* Bounty *from Captain Bligh (Trevor Howard) –* Mutiny on the Bounty *(1962).*

stressed a latent homosexual relationship between Bligh, played by Anthony Hopkins and Christian, played by Mel Gibson. The film was simply called *The Bounty*.

The big money spinner of 1963 (and M-G-M needed it following the losses incurred by *Mutiny on the Bounty*) was *The VIPs*. This was in the Grand Hotel tradition, but its action took place in the international departures lounge at Heathrow Airport in London. The principal story concerned the romantic triangle of a husband and wife (Richard Burton and Elizabeth Taylor) and the wife's lover (Louis Jourdan) with whom she planned to fly away. The fog which has grounded their plane also gives her time to reconsider, and she stays with her husband.

Also waiting for flights are a duchess (Margaret Rutherford, who won the Academy Award for Best Supporting Actress) and a movie producer played by Orson Welles, doing an imitation of Orson Welles. It was a slick film, aided mostly by an impeccable script by Terence Rattigan and sterling direction by Anthony Asquith, and produced at M-G-M British by Anatole de Gruenwald. The romance between Burton and Taylor may have brought people into the theater, but it was the other performers, who also included Maggie Smith, Rod Taylor and Elsa Martinelli, who kept them there.

Cinerama was used a second time in *The Wonderful World of The Brothers Grimm* (1963), a film which intercut a biography of the two German etymologists and collectors of folk tales with several of those tales. Karl Boehm and Laurence

Opposite top: *Laurence Harvey and Karl Boehm in* The Wonderful World of The Brothers Grimm *(1963).*
Opposite below: *Elizabeth Taylor, Richard Burton, Louis Jourdan in* The V.I.P.s *(1963).*

Below: *Sue Lyon and Richard Burton in* The Night of The Iguana *(1964).*
Bottom: *The second episode of* The Yellow Rolls Royce *(1964) starred Shirley MacLaine, George C Scott and Art Carney.*

Harvey starred as the brothers in George Pal's production, which was directed by Henry Levin. The film was shot with the first Cinerama single camera, which eliminated the three projectors previously necessary as well as the visible seams, but it lost the encompassing effect that had made Cinerama as popular as it was in its heyday.

Another big budget triumph was *The Yellow Rolls Royce* (1964), three separate episodes joined by the presence of the magnificent automobile. The first featured Rex Harrison as an English Lord whose wife, Jeanne Moreau, is having an affair with the chauffeur. The second had Shirley MacLaine, as the girl friend of mobster George C Scott, who has a fling with a French guide, Alain Delon. The last episode took place just before World War II and starred Ingrid Bergman as a tourist in Yugoslavia aiding the partisans, led by Omar Sharif. Again Anthony Asquith directed the Anatole de Gruenwald production for M-G-M British.

Director John Huston once again wrote his own screenplay in adapting Tennessee William's play, *The Night of The Iguana* (1964). This starred Richard Burton as T Lawrence Shannon, the defrocked clergyman guiding a busload of school teachers through Mexico. He brings them to the hotel of an old friend, Maxine Faulk (played by Ava Gardner, in one of her finest performances). Also staying there are Hannah Jelkes (Deborah Kerr), a gentle itinerant artist, and her aged grandfather Nonno (Cyril Delevanti), a poet. Shannon is being pursued by a young girl among the tourists, Charlotte

Goodall (Sue Lyon), who has been brought on the trip by Judith Fellowes (Grayson Hall) who harbors a secret lesbian attachment to the younger girl.

Shannon is planning to write to his bishop in hopes of being reinstated, but comes in conflict with Miss Fellowes who plans to press charges for the statutory rape of Charlotte. Angrily he tries to rip off the cross he is wearing in an attempt to convince Miss Fellowes that a man-of-the-cloth would not have become sexually involved. Like the iguana that Maxine keeps tied to the porch, Shannon is at the end of his tether. Hannah gently removes it, and tells him about her own life and how she endures it.

In response to Hannah's kindness in talking him out of his attempt at suicide, Shannon frees the iguana, and accepts his own frailties. The tourists leave, and he remains with Maxine, while Hannah prepares to move on without Nonno who has died in his sleep.

Huston gave Williams the opportunity to read and approve the script before filming, and the result was one of the most accurate translations of the playwright's work to the screen. The entire cast performed brilliantly, but it was Grayson Hall who was nominated for her performance as Judith Fellowes. Once again the public came, drawn by Burton's love scenes, but departed with the appreciation of a marvelous film.

Director Robert Youngson had a surprise success with an 89 minute compilation of clips from previous M-G-M films called *The Big Parade Of Comedy* (1964). This featured such gems from the past as the midnight scene from *Ninotchka*, the Marx Brothers' stateroom scene from *A Night At the*

Opera, as well as a number of Laurel and Hardy skits produced by Hal Roach. The reception of this little film gave impetus to the rising interest in the studio's archives.

Julie Andrews made her M-G-M debut in a role as far from the 'Spoonful of Sugar' image of *Mary Poppins* (Buena Vista, 1964) as possible. This was the war widow in *The Americanization of Emily* (1964), a black comedy featuring James Garner as Charles Madison, the Navy 'dog robber' who by an odd conviction of his Admiral is sent to the Normandy invasion, with the idea of making sure that the first man to die on Omaha Beach is a Navy man. Madison stands for all the anti-war ideologies which were becoming apparent when the film was released. Andrews as Emily Barham, the widow he meets when she is assigned as his driver, has traditional values with regard to war and the military, all the more so since her father was in the Army. The clash of the two as they are falling in love, gives the film its conflict, but its ending with Emily coming over to Madison's way of thinking was pure Hollywood.

The screenplay by Paddy Chayefsky and the direction by Arthur Hiller succeeded because it blended its elements so well. Shot in black and white, the combat scenes were intercut with stock footage for an additional sense of reality.

The cast also included Joyce Grenfell as Emily's mother in a brilliantly embarrassing scene, when Charlie explains his theories of peace and war, not realizing that he is telling her that her entire life and its sacrifices have been in vain. James Coburn also gave a strong performance as the professional Navy man who accompanies Madison on D-Day. Melvyn

Douglas, as usual, was splendid as the Admiral, suffering a nervous breakdown.

The Meredith Willson musical, *The Unsinkable Molly Brown* (1964) was brought to the screen by M-G-M, starring Debbie Reynolds and Harve Presnell, repeating his Broadway role as Molly's husband Johnny. The story of the girl from the mining camp who strikes it rich, becomes a globetrotting millionairess and a heroine of the Titanic sinking, was given a lush production by Lawrence Weingarten and directed by Charles Walters, who had worked with the Freed unit, but it did not start a revival of musicals from the studio. The best known numbers were the raucous 'Belly Up to The Bar, Boys' and 'I Ain't Down Yet.'

The biggest film of 1965 was *Doctor Zhivago*, an adaptation of Boris Pasternak's great novel of the Russian Revolution. More than 25 years after the triumph of *Gone With The Wind*, the studio was still looking for a successor, and felt they had found it with *Zhivago*. The story of a great love set within the background of Russia in transition might have worked, but much of the audience felt that the subject was too foreign and unfamiliar.

Screenwriter Robert Bolt did an amazing job of condensing the novel, and director David Lean gave the film a breadth and drama that actually overpowered the characters.

The vast cast was headed by Omar Sharif as the idealistic poet-doctor, and his two loves were played by Geraldine Chaplin as his wife and childhood friend, Tonya, and Julie Christie as Lara, the army nurse who becomes his muse and great passion. Others in the cast included Sir Ralph Richard-

Right: *Geraldine Chaplin and Omar Sharif as Tonya and Yuri, in* Doctor Zhivago *(1965).*

Opposite top: *James Garner as Charley Madison invades Europe on D-Day in* The Americanization of Emily *(1964).*
Opposite below: *Molly Brown (Debbie Reynolds) celebrates with the miners in* The Unsinkable Molly Brown *(1964).*

son as Tonya's father, Tom Courtenay as the young revolutionary, Pasha, and Rod Steiger as Komarovsky, the government minister who first seduces Lara.

Though Bolt and Lean set out to put the Russian Revolution into context anyone could understand, the subject was too vast. The audience had to have some background understanding to comprehend the severity of the changes that were telecoped to allow the entire novel to be covered. The spectacle, however, was breathtaking, from charges across the snowy streets of Moscow to charges across the snowy steppes. Lean was able to use his crowds well, almost as another character, rather like the chorus in *Boris Godunov*. The crowd are as one when as disgruntled troops they turn on and trample their officers, or as peasants take possession of the great house of Tonya's father, leaving the family only a few rooms.

The photography by Freddie Young was also notable, especially in the winter scenes at the country house where Zhivago and Lara come together for the last time. The music by Maurice Jarre, which including the popular 'Lara's Theme,' ('Somewhere My Love') added immensely to the film, and received one of the four Academy Awards won by *Dr Zhivago*, which also included costume design, screenplay and cinematography.

The best things about *Grand Prix* (1966) were definitely the racing sequences. Directed by John Frankenheimer, these were full of heart-pounding action, intercut with driver and fan reaction. By comparison the rather predictable involvements of the cast, including James Garner, Yves Montand and Eva Marie Saint, were a bit boring in the screenplay by Robert Alan Arthur.

One of the most curious films distributed by M-G-M was Michelangelo Antonioni's *Blow-Up* (1967), a contrast of reality and surreality, which left the audience wondering what it had actually seen. The film covered 24 hours in the life of a young fashion photographer (David Hemmings) while he finishes an assignment with a writhing model (Verushka), takes candid pictures in the park, or rolls around on some no-seam paper with two aspiring models. The pictures in the park prove a mystery when a woman (Vanessa Redgrave) asks for the negatives, and the photographer in enlarging the prints perceives a body in them.

It has been felt that the body, and supposed murder, are Antonioni's McGuffins, the unexplained object of a quest. The audience knows only what the photographer knows, and sees only what the photographer sees.

The film owed some of its success to the nude scenes and the ambience of 'swinging' London, which was brilliantly captured by cameraman Carlo di Palma.

It is said that Francois Duvalier, the dictator of Haiti, known

Right: *David Hemmings finds a mysterious detail in one of his photographs in* Blow-Up *(1967).*

Opposite: *The Russian Army rebels against its officers during World War I, in* Dr Zhivago *(1965).*
Below: *James Garner and Brian Bedford were drivers in* Grand Prix *(1966). Jessica Walter played Bedford's wife.*

as Papa Doc, was so incensed by the vision of his country portrayed in *The Comedians* (1967), based on the novel by Graham Greene, that he had voodoo images made of the stars, Richard Burton, Elizabeth Taylor and Alec Guinness, and stuck pins in them. The film was actually made in Dahomey and the South of France, fortunately for the safety of both the cast and crew.

The plot of *The Comedians* brings together a British hotel-owner (Burton), an ambassador and his wife (Peter Ustinov and Miss Taylor) and a con-man (Alec Guinness), who claims to be a member of the British Secret Service. This unusual group become isolated by an attempted coup involving James Earl Jones and George Stanford Brown. Also present are two well-meaning tourists, brilliantly played by Paul Ford and Lillian Gish, who cannot believe the horrors they have heard about, until they accidentally witness a public beheading.

The direction was by Peter Glenville, and the script was adapted by the author. The lush photography was the province of Henri Decae, who caught the atmosphere of a poor tropical country, still retaining some aspects of its colonial past to perfection.

Like many war movies before it, *The Dirty Dozen* (1967) described an Allied mission behind enemy lines. What made it different were the men involved. Major Reisman (Lee Marvin) is instructed to train 12 hardened criminals for the mission, because headquarters believes that such men are expendable.

The group is a cracked-mirror image of the usual heroic band: a simple-minded southerner, a black, a Puerto Rican, a

tough guy from Brooklyn. The training of this band takes up one part of the film, while the execution of the mission is the second, and more important half. Another change from previous films of such exploits is the sheer violence and bloodthirstiness with which the band carries out its mission, which concludes with a massive explosion.

The cast, headed by Marvin, lifted what might have been a rather ordinary war movie into a different sphere. John Cassavetes was nominated as Best Supporting Actor for his performance as the psychotic hustler, Franko. Also memorable were Telly Savalas as the sadistic killer, Archer Maggott; Donald Sutherland as the retarded Vernon Pinkley; and Charles Bronson as the only sympathetic member of the squad, Wadislaw. The director was Robert Aldrich, and the film became the big box office winner for the year.

Another genre film with a difference was *Welcome to Hard Times* (1967), a Western starring Henry Fonda. Hard Times was a town under siege by a gunman (Aldo Ray) until the townspeople, led by a nervous Fonda, manage to oust him. The film, directed by Burt Kennedy, who wrote the script based on the novel by E L Doctorow, also starred Janice Rule and Keenan Wynn.

Space has held a fascination for movie-makers since Georges Méliès' *A Trip To The Moon* (1902), but nothing had prepared audiences for Stanley Kubrick's *2001: A Space Odyssey* (1968). The film had its genesis in a short story by Arthur C Clarke called 'The Sentinel,' which concerned an alien artifact found on the moon. This became only one of the bizarre episodes in a film which made a popular hit out of Richard Strauss' tone poem 'Also Sprach Zarathustra.'

The film had a impact that the subsequent years have not lessened, principally because it does leave so many questions unanswered, though a clue may be found in the full title. An odyssey is, after all, a quest.

The beginning of the film seems a perfectly straightforward projection of the discovery of the awareness of tools

Above: *A stewardess on the lunar shuttle in* 2001: A Space Odyssey *(1968).*
Right: *The Dirty Dozen (1967) included James Brown, John Cassavetes, Telly Savalas, Charles Bronson and George Kennedy.*

Opposite top: *Henry Fonda in the ruins of the town he has defended in* Welcome to Hard Times *(1967).*
Opposite below: *Richard Burton, James Earl Jones, Alec Guinness, Elizabeth Taylor and Peter Ustinov starred in* The Comedians *(1967).*

by primitive primates, which led to the use of the tool as a weapon in a battle for precedence at a life-giving waterhole in the arid climate of the new planet Earth. This concept is instantly dismissed by the appearance of a great black monolith. Is it that which triggers the killer instinct in the ape-like creatures?

Many eons in the future, i.e. the late twentieth century, a moon shuttle is bearing a party of scientists to a lunar excavation, where a similar monolith has been found. Questions are asked by Soviet scientists in an orbiting way station, where the audience is granted glimpses of current life. But once at the site, the expedition is destroyed.

In the year 2001, a great space ship is taking a small crew of scientists on a probe to Jupiter. The two astronauts who are not in a state of suspended animation work with the computer HAL, who controls the fragile support system of the ship, as well as any number of functions. For no explained reason HAL suggests that an antenna for the radio system connecting the ship to earth is malfunctioning. While an astronaut is repairing it, HAL, of his own volition, lets him loose in space, effectively killing him. When the second astronaut tries to retrieve the body, HAL will not reopen the doors for reentry. Desperately, the astronaut blasts his way through an emergency port. He finds that HAL has disconnected the life-support systems of the three in suspended

animation and they, too, are dead. Desperately, he deprograms the machine, and takes over manual control of the ship, which continues on its isolated way to Jupiter, where he spots another vast monolith before his ship encounters the turbulence that surrounds the planet and moves him into the unknown.

It is this last section that has given rise to so much speculation about this film. The audience is bombarded with high contrast landscapes in shifting colors at high speeds and suddenly finds itself in a room with the astronaut, who steps out of his pod, grows old, and dies in the great Louis XVI bed which dominates the room, with a black monolith at his feet. The final image is that of a fetus, floating in the womb, or is it space?

Kubrick's evocations of the future world are extraordinary, because they are believable. Telephone transmission can be effected by the use of a plastic card. Furniture and clothing are acceptably modern, although the stewardesses' uniforms on the moon shuttle, which were designed by Hardy Amies, have dated badly.

Keir Dullea and Gary Lockwood, as the two astronauts, are completely unemotional, as if their training has overwhelmed their personalities. Even when planning to disconnect HAL, a conspiracy HAL divines by reading their lips when they think they are safe in a soundproof pod, there is

no emotion. The only emotion belongs to HAL, whose voice was provided by Douglas Rain, whose dying is rather like a return to the machine's childhood, as it whispers 'Daisy, Daisy, give me your answer do . . .' The acronym HAL, which is said to stand for Heuristically Programed Algorithmic Computer, was derived by Kubrick by dropping back one letter in the alphabet from IBM.

The special effects which won an Academy Award were supervised by Kubrick. The space ships were an elaborate set of miniatures, the effect of floating in space created by shooting below an actor suspended on piano wire. The turning set, first employed by Fred Astaire in *Royal Wedding* (1950), was again brought into use.

As if to prove that the studio suffered from the continuing change of people in authority, the bulk of the M-G-M films of 1969 were poorly received or remarkably pretentious. The big moneymaker, *Where Eagles Dare*, was an adaptation of a thriller by Alistair MacLean, starred Richard Burton and Clint Eastwood as Allied agents infiltrating a Nazi stronghold to rescue a captured general. The plot also contained so many double-crosses that the audience was never quite sure who was on which side. Mary Ure (who incidentally had costarred with Burton in *Look Back In Anger* (GB, 1959), and Ingrid Pitt provided the romantic interrest, and Brian G Hutton directed.

M-G-M British also produced a musical remake of *Goodbye Mr Chips* (1969) starring Peter O'Toole and Petula Clark in the roles originated by Robert Donat and Greer Garson. The score by Leslie Bricusse had no hits, and the direction by Herbert Ross, though good, struck no emotion in the modern audience. The following year, M-G-M closed their British studio and went into partnership with EMI for the production of films in Great Britain.

Ryan's Daughter (1970) was David Lean's first film after *Dr Zhivago*. Set in Ireland during the Troubles, it was the story of a willful girl (Sarah Miles) who marries the local schoolmaster (Robert Mitchum), without understanding him or what marriage entails. When a new officer (Christopher

Above: *Peter O'Toole (in cap and gown) starred in the musical remake of* Goodbye Mr Chips *(1969).*
Opposite: *Astronauts Gary Lockwood (left) and Keir Dullea discuss HAL's possible malfunction in* 2001: A Space Odyssey *(1968).*

Right: *The special spy team of* Where Eagles Dare *(1969) included Clint Eastwood, Richard Burton, Mary Ure and (right) Ingrid Pitt and Patrick Wymark.*

Jones) who is suffering from shell-shock from his experiences in the trenches, joins the local garrison, she falls in love with him.

Filmed mainly on the Dingle Peninsula in the Republic of Ireland, the movie was visually superb, especially a beach scene of the villagers unloading contraband guns during a storm. The treatment may have been too spectacular for the story, which concerned rather small people in an emotional triangle that was entirely removed from the political consequences of the period, although Sarah Miles was tarred and had her head shaved by the women of the village for consorting with the enemy.

The outstanding performances were John Mills as the village idiot, which won him the Academy Award for Best Supporting Actor, and Trevor Howard as the local priest. Freddie Young's superlative photography was also honored by the Academy.

In 1971 M-G-M declared its highest net income for 25 years, but over half that amount came from the disposal of assets, including the tremendous prop and costume collections. Even the sketches which had been taped to the walls of both departments went under the auctioneer's hammer, along with Dorothy's ruby slippers, Rhett Butler's beaver hat, and Andy Hardy's jalopy. It was the end of an era.

M-G-M bought the film rights to Sandy Wilson's endearing little musical *The Boy Friend* in 1956, but had difficulty in developing a script which would not overcome the simplicity of the story. In 1971, they released the movie version which had set out to do precisely that.

Directed by Ken Russell, who also reworked the script, *The Boy Friend* (1971) was now a loving conglomeration of the backstage musical and the original show. It starred ex-model Twiggy as the clumsy assistant stage manager, who has to go on for the star (Glenda Jackson, in a cameo) when she breaks

Opposite: *Father Collins (Trevor Howard) and Michael, the village idiot (John Mills) attempt to land a curragh in* Ryan's Daughter *(1970).*

Right: The Boy Friend *(1971) was filled with dance numbers performed and filmed as a tribute to Busby Berkeley.*
Below: *Assistant stage manager Twiggy wistfully eyes the show's star Christopher Gable in* The Boy Friend *(1971).*

an ankle. However, it is not Broadway, and it is not opening night. It is a matinee in an English industrial town.

Much of the fun came from Russell's manner of elaborating the musical numbers in the manner of Busby Berkeley, and some was due to the charm of all the performers, including Christopher Gable as the male lead, on whom Twiggy has always had a crush, and Tommy Tune as one of the chorus boys who performs a mean Charleston with Antonia Ellis.

Most of Sandy Wilson's score was left intact, and didn't suffer from Russell's treatment. 'I Could Be Happy With You,' 'Sur La Plage,' 'All I Want is a Room in Bloomsbury' and 'Poor Little Pierrette' were all turned into tremendous chorus numbers involving vast sets and scores of dancers. Unfortunately, the public seemed unaware of Russell's intent, and even word-of-mouth could not save it at the box office.

An entirely different M-G-M release was also British. The Royal Ballet's film version of its full length ballet, *Peter Rabbit and Tales of Beatrix Potter*, with choreography by Sir Frederick Ashton, was a tale within a tale. The first dances were seen against the background of Potter's Victorian childhood, as she taught herself to draw small animals. In the first ballet sequence, the lovely and funny 'Tale of the Two Bad Mice,' the audience is taken into a child's doll house, which is systematically destroyed by the two rodents Hunca Munca and Tom Thumb. The episode concludes with a charming mouse waltz.

When the child Beatrix is taken to the Cumberland countryside for the summer, the dance episodes include, 'The Tale of Jemima Puddleduck,' 'The Tale of Squirrel Nutkin' and 'The Tale of Little Pig Robinson,' which includes a beautiful *pas de deux* performed by both dancers in toe shoes (a

Above: *In the finale of* Peter Rabbit and Tales of Beatrix Potter *(1971), Johnny Town Mouse and his country cousins enjoy a picnic.*

Right: *Shaft (Richard Roundtree) is menaced by a hoodlum (Edmund Hashim) in* Shaft *(1971), one of the first thrillers to feature a black hero.*

first for a male dancer). Other enchanting vignettes include 'The Tale of Jeremy Fisher,' as the dancer leaps like a frog, and the lovely finale which brings on many of the beloved characters, including Mrs Tiggie-Winkle, danced by Sir Frederick Ashton.

The wonderful masks by Rostislav Doboujinsky truly gave the dancers the appearance of animals, and the score, compiled from many old English dance tunes and folk melodies, was composed by John Lanchbery. The director was Reginald Mills and the producers John Brabourne and Richard Goodwin. It was one of the most successful depictions of ballet on film.

A new trend in films was evident with the success of *Shaft* (1971), one of the first all-black crime dramas. Based on the novel by Ernest Tidyman and directed by Gordon Parks, the film starred Richard Roundtree as the black private eye, up against a Harlem racketeer, played by Moses Gunn. The Oscar-winning theme by Isaac Hayes enticed people into the theater to a better-than-average detective thriller. Its success foretold the rise of black-sploitation.

Nineteen seventy-three marked the last year of M-G-M as a major distributor, as the studio liquidated its overseas theaters and the music companies which had cost almost more to run than they brought in in profits. For the next ten years, the M-G-M films would be distributed by United Artists in the United States and Canada, and Cinema International Corporation, who already handled overseas rights for Universal and Paramount, for the rest of the world.

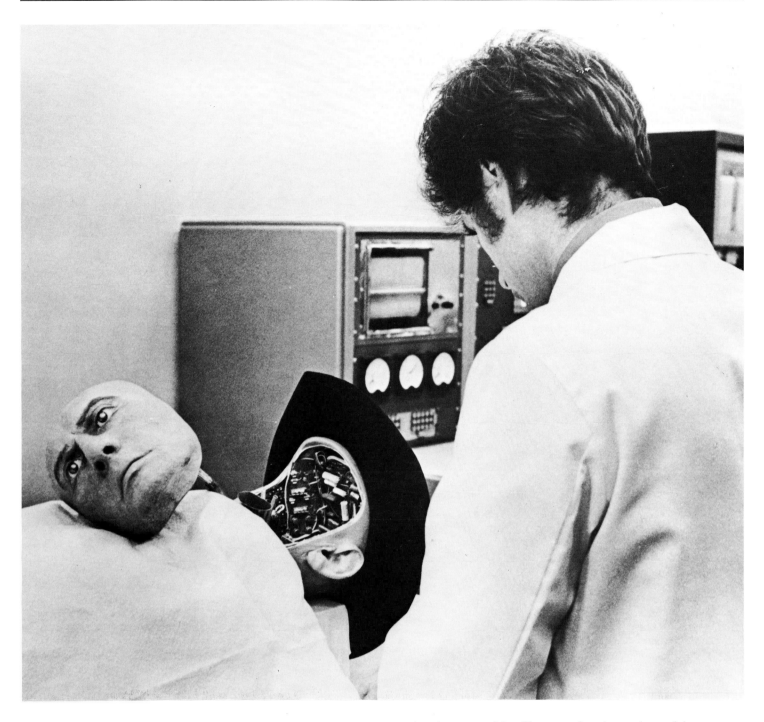

The gunfighter robot (Yul Brynner) in WestWorld *(1973) is reprogrammed.*

Before that end, M-G-M had produced and distributed *WestWorld* (1973), a science-fiction film with western overtones. Set in an amusement park of the future, which offers three alternatives, Roman World, Medieval World and West-World, the vacation chosen by two friends Richard Benjamin and James Brolin. At WestWorld, they are garbed as cowboys, sent out into a western town to drink, carouse and, if they like, shoot it up. The weapons they carry will only deactivate the robots who inhabit the park for the amusement, sexual or otherwise, of the visitors. One of the guests, Richard Benjamin, gets into a showdown with a black-shirted robot, played by Yul Brynner, and 'kills' him. The robot is returned to the park after maintenance and resetting, but something has gone wrong, for the robot shoots and kills Brolin, and then comes after Benjamin. All over the parks, the robots have gone haywire. After temporarily disengaging the robot, Benjamin escapes.

The director of the film was also the author of the screenplay, Michael Crichton, who managed to maintain the believable suspense until the robots ran amok. The effects however, were tremendous, especially in the maintenance sheds where the robots are sent along an assembly line to have limbs removed and replaced, and are recharged. Brynner was wonderfully sinister as the gunfighter.

The most popular film of 1974 was Jack Haley Jr's production of *That's Entertainment*, a loving compilation of clips from great M-G-M films from the past. Though dismissed by some as 'dancing on the grave' or 'something to be expected from a studio which had stooped to suck marrow from the bones of its past glory,' the film gave many people their first opportunity to see some of the stars and musical numbers that had made M-G-M the studio it had been.

Introduced by eleven members of the M-G-M stock company, including Fred Astaire, Gene Kelly, Frank Sinatra and Elizabeth Taylor, were numbers that dated back to *The Hollywood Revue of 1929*. Included were such show stoppers as 'A Pretty Girl Is Like a Melody' from *The Great*

That's Entertainment *(1974)* *featured highlights from the studio's past, including (above) Marge and Gower Champion in* Showboat *(1951), (left) Joan Crawford and Paul Gibbons* sing *'Gotta Feelin' For You' in* Hollywood Revue of 1929 *(1929) and (opposite) Gene Kelly and Fred Astaire in 'The Babbitt and The Bromide' from* The Great Ziegfeld *(1936).*

Ziegfeld (1936) 'Abba Daba Honeymoon' from *Two Weeks with Love* (1950) and a selection of production numbers from Esther Williams' *Million Dollar Mermaid* (1952) and *Bathing Beauty* (1944).

Liza Minnelli introduced a selection of her mother Judy Garland's songs beginning with the two-reeler she made with Deanna Durbin called *Every Sunday* (1936), and the 'Dear Mr Gable' number from *Broadway Melody of 1938* (1937), which dissolved into a well selected compilation of Gable in many of his most famous roles. The film concluded with a selection of the complete numbers from some of the most successful Arthur Freed musicals: 'Hallelujah' from *Hit The Deck* (1955); the Barn-Raising Ballet from *Seven Brides for Seven Brothers* (1954), 'Gigi' and 'Thank Heaven for Little Girls' from *Gigi* (1958) and the complete ballet from *An American in Paris* (1951).

Fifty years after its founding, M-G-M was drawing on its past, because it was uncertain about its future. The following year it was back in production.

REBIRTH

THE SUDDEN RISE IN M-G-M profits was due only in part to feature films. The bulk of it came from the company's newest asset, the vast M-G-M Grand Hotel in Las Vegas, Nevada. The demand for new films was increasing, and without the distribution network, the studio could concentrate on making films, leaving the headaches of distributing them to United Artists.

In the footsteps of *That's Entertainment* (1974) came *That's Entertainment, Part II* (1975), one of the more successful sequels of the era. This time the producers were David Melnick and Saul Chaplin, who had done much of the scoring for the Freed musicals in the old days.

It is a tribute to M-G-M that their archives could produce another selection of material almost as good as that in the first film. Introduced by Fred Astaire and Gene Kelly, who danced together for the first time since 'The Babbitt and the Bromide,' in *The Ziegfeld Follies* (1945), in a specially choreographed opening number, the film included great dance numbers like 'For Me and My Gal' from the film of the same name (1942), danced by Kelly, and 'I Love The Look Of You,' from *Silk Stockings* (1957) with Astaire and Cyd Charisse, and also gave time to non-musical stars.

A clip from *The Pirate* (1948), with Kelly and the Nicholas Brothers, 'Be A Clown,' segued into a tribute to a number of the clowns who had worked for the studio – Abbott and Costello, Jimmy Durante, Buster Keaton and the Marx Brothers, who were shown in the stateroom scene from *A Night At The Opera* (1935).

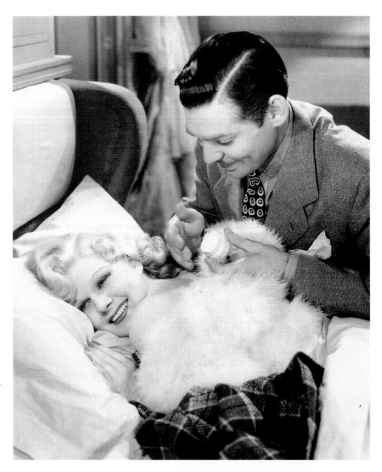

Previous spread: *'The Broadway Melody' finale from* Singin' in the Rain *was used in* That's Entertainment II *(1975).*
Opposite top: *Included in* That's Entertainment II *(1975) were scenes with Clark Gable and Jean Harlow from Harlow's last film,* Saratoga *(1937).*
Right: *Sean Connery starred as Raisulli, 'the last of the Barbary pirates' and Candice Bergen as Mrs Pedacaris, his hostage, in* The Wind and the Lion *(1975).*

Opposite bottom: *A number with Cyd Charisse and Fred Astaire in* Silk Stockings *(1957), the musical version of* Ninotchka *(1939), was featured in* That's Entertainment II *(1975).*
Below: *Veteran vaudevillians Walter Matthau (left) and George Burns revive their act for television in* The Sunshine Boys *(1975).*

A short subject of 1929 called *The Song Writer's Revue* featured composer Nacio Herb Brown singing his own 'The Wedding of The Painted Doll,' from *Broadway Melody* (1929). That scene dissolved into the number itself. The others featured the numerous musical biographies produced by the studio from *Words and Music* (1948, Rodgers and Hart) to *The Great Waltz* (1938, Johann Strauss, the Younger). Greta Garbo was heard saying 'I just vant to be alone,' Gable was heard saying 'I love ya',' in *Saratoga* (1937) and Hedy Lamarr reminded the audience that 'They call me Tondelayo' in *White Cargo* (1942).

Chevalier singing 'I'm going to Maxim's,' from *The Merry Widow* (1934) introduced a tribute to Paris and the musicals set there: *Gigi* (1959), *An American in Paris* (1951) and part of *Till the Clouds Roll By* (1946). Also included were 'Gotta Dance,' from *The Bandwagon* (1953), 'I Remember It Well,' from *Gigi* and 'There's No Business Like Show Business,' from *Annie Get Your Gun* (1950).

A new venture in producing came about when M-G-M shared production with its once arch-rival, Columbia, for *The Wind And The Lion* (1975). This old fashioned adventure based on a true incident starred Sean Connery and Candice Bergen in turn-of-the-century Morocco. Connery played a Berber tribesman who kidnaps and holds for ransom Eden Pedacaris, an American widow (Bergen), and her children. Brian Keith costarred as President Theodore Roosevelt and John Huston played his Secretary of State, John Hay. John Milius directed his own screenplay. The film was a surprising success, and Connery was superb as Raisulli, 'the last of the Barbary pirates.' By the end of the film, the audience is as enthralled with Raisulli as Mrs Pedacaris is. History tells us Eden Pedacaris was a man, but when did M-G-M ever let history interfere with a good plot?

Neil Simon's Broadway hit *The Sunshine Boys* (1975) came to the screen with Walter Matthau and George Burns, who

Left: *Marsha Mason and Richard Dreyfuss as the unwilling roommates who fall in love in* The Goodbye Girl *(1977).*

Bottom left: *Faye Dunaway won an Academy Award for her performance as the ambitious producer in* Network *(1976).*
Opposite: *Irene Cara and Lee Curreri (right) played two of the talented students at New York's School of the Performing Arts in* Fame *(1980).*

was returning to the movies after 40 years, in a part written for Jack Benny, who regrettably died before filming began.

Burns and Matthau were wonderful as the two vaudeville partners whose love-hate relationship keeps them going. Richard Benjamin co-starred as Matthau's eager nephew who is planning to revive their act for television. The director, Herbert Ross, and producer, Ray Stark, shot it primarily on location in New York. Burns won the Academy Award for Best Supporting Actor, in a year otherwise given over to *One Flew Over The Cuckoo's Nest* (UA, 1975).

Network (1976) was one of the first films to examine the television industry, which had done so much to hasten the demise of the old studio system, and it did so in a devastating manner. The withering screenplay by Paddy Chayefsky focused on the greed and search for power in network television, contrasting the methods of a middle-aged executive and younger woman who was pushing her way to the top.

The catalyst is the news commentator, played by Peter Finch, who announces his firing on camera and follows up by informing the television audience that he will kill himself on camera at the end of his last show. That announcement grips the audience's morbid imagination, and the man becomes the spokesman for all the disgruntled elements in the world. He is also led on by the powers that be, and eventually is killed on camera.

With Finch in *Network* were William Holden as the executive; Faye Dunaway, at her most predatory, as the ambitious producer; Robert Duvall, as cold blooded as ever as the vice president from the conglomerate who had taken over the network; and Ned Beatty as the chairman of the board.

Chayefsky's script kept within the realm of believability even with his satirizing the ultimate news spectacular, which included a mystic who would foretell the news of tomorrow. Sidney Lumet, the director, managed to keep the plot from seeming too fantastic. Dunaway, Chayefsky and Finch were all honored with Academy Awards, but sadly Mr Finch's was posthumous, as he died during a publicity campaign for the film.

Neil Simon had another winner with *The Goodbye Girl* (1977), a co-production with Warner Bros. Starring Marsha Mason and Richard Dreyfuss, the comedy told of a young divorcée who comes home to find that her husband has rented his share of the apartment to a total stranger, an actor played by Dreyfuss. Their antagonism turns to affection, and when he gets his big break and leaves for Hollywood, she prepares to follow. Quinn Cummings was exceptional as Mason's young daughter, and Dreyfuss, who won the Academy Award for Best Actor, had a wonderful time, especially in the scene where he plays Shakespeare's Richard III in a high camp fashion. Like *The Sunshine Boys* (1975), the film was directed by Herbert Ross.

In May 1980, the studio regained some autonomy when the vast corporation was split into M-G-M Grand Hotels Inc. and Metro Goldwyn Mayer Film Company. Twenty million dollars were spent on studio improvements, though very few films were completed that year.

One that was, was probably the best and most original musical since the fifties. This was *Fame* (1980), a film about the loves and ambitions of eight students at New York's High School of Performing Arts. Directed by Alan Parker, the young cast sang and danced its way about the New York locations. The film won two Academy Awards, for Best Musical Score and Best Song ('Fame,' written by Michael Gore and Dean Pitchford). The sequel was a long-running television series with some of the young stars repeating their movie roles.

Richard Dreyfuss appeared in *Whose Life Is It Anyway?* (1981), the story of a sculptor who is paralyzed from the neck down in an automobile accident. Brian Clark and Reginald Rose adapted Clark's play, which had been a surprise hit in both London and New York, opening up the action to make the film less of a hospital drama. John Cassavetes and Christine Lahti costarred as the doctors, and the director was John Badham.

Above: *Steve Martin in one of the elaborate musical numbers that punctuate* Pennies From Heaven *(1981).*
Opposite: *Kevin Bacon, Mickey Rourke, Daniel Stern and Paul Reiser in one of their sessions in* Diner *(1982).*

Left: *Peter O'Toole as the swashbuckling actor, Alan Swann, with Mark-Linn Baker and Jessica Harper in* My Favorite Year *(1982).*

Another offbeat production was *Pennies From Heaven* (1981), starring Steve Martin. This was based on a British television series about the dreary lives of a couple during the Depression, but writer Dennis Potter opened up the drama by the insertion of big production numbers to original thirties recordings which were lip-synced by the cast, which also included Jessica Harper as Martin's wife and Bernadette Peters as his mistress. Among the old recordings used to such effect were Rudy Vallee's 'Life Is Just A Bowl Of Cherries,' Bing Crosby's 'Did You Ever See A Dream Walking,' Fred Astaire's 'Let's Face The Music' and 'Pennies From Heaven' sung by Arthur Tracy, 'The Street Singer.' Herbert Ross was the director.

An unusually personal view of divorce and its toll on the children of a failed marriage was found in *Shoot The Moon* (1982), starring Diane Keaton and Albert Finney as the ideal couple whose world comes apart. After a separation, the wife begins an affair with a younger man, one that her eldest daughter develops a crush on. The screenplay by Bo Goldman and the direction by Alan Parker avoided an explanation of the failure of the marriage and concentrated on the division itself. The four children were played by Dana Hill, Viveka Davis, Tracey Gold and Tina Yothers. Albert Finney was brilliant as the man trying to keep the affection of his children in a situation that he has helped to create, but is uncertain how.

A different look at television was available in the charming comedy, *My Favorite Year* (1982). Mark Linn-Baker was the young comedy writer given the task of minding swashbuckling film star Alan Swann (Peter O'Toole) when he is scheduled for a guest appearance on the King Kaiser Show. Though Swann freezes when he becomes aware that television is 'live,' he is persuaded to go on to the defense of the television star when a skit is interrupted by the mobsters who have taken a dim view of seeing the boss lampooned on network television. Together Swann and Kaiser are able to defeat the mob to an ovation by the studio audience.

O'Toole was simply magnificent as Swann and the role earned him another Academy Award nomination, but the rest of the cast was not far behind. Joseph Bologna played King Kaiser, veteran screen writer Adolph Green appeared as the show's producer and Lainie Kazan had a wonderful cameo as Mark Linn-Baker's mother. It was a most affectionate tribute to the Golden Age of television.

Another film with a sense of nostalgia was *Diner* (1982), a film about growing up in the fifties. Five friends, played by a sterling cast of young actors (Steve Guttenberg, Daniel Stern, Mickey Rourke, Kevin Bacon and Timothy Daly), maintain their high school friendships with nightly bull sessions in a Baltimore diner, and these talks have become the central core of their lives.

The early audience reaction on the West Coast to *Diner* was poor, but certain critics were very impressed with it, and forced the studio to release it again in the East, where it became an instant hit through word of mouth. Director Barry Levinson also wrote the screenplay.

Steven Spielberg wrote and produced *Poltergeist* (1982), but the director was Tobe Hooper. It was the story of a house inhabited by evil spirits that disrupt the family with mysterious incidents before the youngest child, who is the only one that can sense them, is abducted by the spirits. After calling in a team of parapsychologists and a psychic, the child is rescued, but the family escapes only moments before the house implodes.

There are a number of wonderful Spielberg touches: the presence of the spirits in a snowy television set, the piling up of furniture as if by magic, insects which attack only members of the family.

The stars included Craig T Nelson and Jobeth Williams as the parents, Beatrice Straight as the head of the parapsychologists and Zelda Rubenstein as the mystic. The children, especially Heather O'Rourke, were exceptional, as were the special effects by Industrial Light and Magic.

One of the biggest hits of the year was *Victor/Victoria* (1982), a comedy based on the German film *Viktor und Viktoria* (UFA, 1934) about a girl who can get a singing job only by posing as a transvestite. In another role distant from Mary Poppins, Julie Andrews played the part beautifully, and she was ably assisted by Robert Preston as the homosexual who helps her get the job and James Garner as the Chicago mobster who is afraid that his interest in the young 'man' means that he has strange tendencies. The biggest surprise was Lesley Ann Warren as Garner's mistress. Blake Edwards directed and wrote the screenplay. Andrews, Preston and Warren were all nominated for Academy Awards.

Just in time for Christmas of 1982 came *A Christmas Story*, an adaptation of an episode in Jean Shepherd's book of reminiscences, *In God We Trust, All Others Pay Cash*. Peter Billingsley played the young boy who wanted the Red Ryder air rifle, and his parents were played by Melinda Dillon and Darren McGavin. The direction was by Bob Clark, whose most popular film had been the puerile *Porky's*.

Another film with a young cast was *War Games* (1983), about a young computer hacker who manages to break into the Pentagon system and calls up a nuclear strike, thinking he is playing a new game called 'Thermonuclear War.' The young man was played by Matthew Broderick and Ally Sheedy played his girlfriend. Together the two go looking for John Wood, the scientist who created the program, and is the only man who can dismantle it. The movie's director was John Badham.

The director of *Yentl* (1983) was also the star, Barbra Streisand, who also worked on the screenplay with Jack Rosenthal. Based on a story by Isaac Bashevis Singer, *Yentl* tells of a young Jewish girl who disguises herself as a boy when her father (Nehemiah Persoff) dies, so that she can attend the Hebrew school which is closed to women. She falls in love with a fellow student (Mandy Patinkin) who thinks she is a man, and arranges her marriage to the beautiful Amy Irving. Streisand put her whole heart into the project, which was well done, but was not the critical or popular success she hoped and expected it to be. The musical score by Michel Legrand and Alan and Marilyn Bergman did win an Academy Award.

Top right: *Matthew Broderick and Ally Sheedy play Thermonuclear War in* War Games *(1983).*
Right: *Mandy Patinkin (left) and Barbra Streisand in* Yentl *(1983).*

Opposite top: *Julie Andrews and Robert Preston starred in* Victor/Victoria *(1982) as the transvestite singer, Victoria, and her homosexual advisor, Toddy.*
Opposite bottom: *Parents Craig T Nelson and Jo Beth Williams are curious about the beings their daughter Heather O'Rourke senses in the television in* Poltergeist *(1982).*

One of the best films of the year was made in Australia, but released through M-G-M. This was *The Year of Living Dangerously* (1983), directed by Peter Weir and starring Mel Gibson as an Australian journalist in Indonesia in the last years of Sukarno's regime. Sigourney Weaver costarred as the English embassy secretary who tries not to become involved with him, but the picture was stolen by Linda Hunt as the Eurasian dwarf, Billy Kwan, who is the journalist's photographer. Miss Hunt, who played the part of a man, won the Academy Award for the Best Supporting Actress.

Nineteen eighty-four was the year that *2010* was released. Billed as a sequel to *2001: A Space Odyssey*, it was, rather, the story of a different expedition which called for US and Soviet collaboration to rescue another mission. It starred Roy Scheider, John Lithgow and Helen Mirren. Keir Dullea, who had starred in the first film, was also featured, and the movie was produced, directed and written by Peter Hyams.

A major change had come over M-G-M in 1981, when the studio bought United Artists, which had been founded in 1919 by Charlie Chaplin, Douglas Fairbanks, Mary Pickford and D W Griffith. In the package came the rights to all the films of United Artists, which included the lucrative James Bond and Pink Panther series. This in turn led to the issue of two films, *The Trail of the Pink Panther* (1982) and *The Curse of the Pink Panther* (1984), using clips and outtakes. Though not critical successes, the public loved them. Another new asset was the *Rocky* pictures of Sylvester Stallone. The package also included all the pre-1950 features of Warner Brothers, which had been bought by United Artists Television, and the valuable musical library which included M-G-M's own, sold to United Artists in 1973.

United Artists would continue to produce films and television programs as a separate entity from M-G-M and act as distributor for the United States and Canada. The overseas distribution would be handled by a new company, United International Pictures, formed by MGM/UA together with Universal and Paramount.

Above: *Australian reporter Guy Hamilton (Mel Gibson) holds photographer Billy Kwan (Linda Hunt) on his shoulders to record the riots in* The Year of Living Dangerously *(1983).*

Bottom left: *Grace Jones as May Day, one of James Bond's most unusual adversaries, in* A View to a Kill (1985).

Below: *John Lithgow and Roy Scheider as astronauts in* 2010 *(1984).*

In 1985 M-G-M released *That's Dancin'* (1985), another anthology put together by Jack Haley, Jr and David Niven, Jr that contained clips of famous dance sequences, including rare footage of Isadora Duncan, and a wonderful unfamiliar number by the Nicholas Brothers, as well as better known dances by better known stars which had not already been included in both *That's Entertainment* compilations. Segments were introduced by Gene Kelly, Liza Minnelli, Ray Bolger, Mikhail Baryshnikov, and Sammy Davis, Jr.

A View To A Kill (1985), starring Roger Moore and Grace Jones, was the first James Bond film to be produced under the new MGM/UA distribution agreement. It was also the last time (to date) that Moore was to play the never aging spy. This time his nemesis was an evil industrialist named Max Zorin, played by Christopher Walken. Jones costarred as Zorin's hit woman, May Day. The usual dazzling scenery included an iceberg, the Eiffel Tower and the Golden Gate Bridge.

Another major film was *To Live And Die In LA* (1985), directed by William Friedkin, who had won an Academy Award for *The French Connection* (20th Century-Fox, 1971). The film starred William Petersen as a Secret Service agent trying to avenge his partner who had been killed by a counterfeiter, played with his usual demented menace by Willem Dafoe. The film, written by Friedkin and Irving H. Levin, featured a heart-stopping car chase against four lanes of traffic on an LA freeway.

Wise Guys (1986), directed by Brian DePalma, starred Danny DeVito and Joe Piscopo as two bumbling gangsters from Newark who accidentally double-cross the mob boss at a horse race, and are set up by him to kill one another. The comedy, with a screenplay by George Gallo, was enhanced by wonderful performances by the supporting cast which included Harvey Keitel, Dan Hedaya, Patti LuPone, and wrestler Captain Lou Albano as the mob enforcer, 'Mr Fixer.'

Another 'buddy movie' released by M-G-M in 1986 was *Running Scared*, starring Billy Crystal and Gregory Hines as two cops on the verge of retirement. Directed by Peter Hyams and written by Gary Devore and Jimmy Huston, the film worked best when the relationship of the two cops took center screen, although there was a good chase sequence with a cab and limousine on the Chicago El tracks, and a scary denouement in the atrium of the State of Illinois Center.

It was a wonder that any films had been released under the M-G-M banner at all in 1986. In March, Ted Turner bought the company for $1.5 billion dollars. Two months later, he sold the M-G-M film lot to Lorimar television and the name and 'Leo the Lion' logo back to Las Vegas entrepreneur Kirk Kerkorian, who had taken control in 1969. Turner retained the enormous M-G-M film library, which also included that of United Artists and the pre-1950 Warner Brothers films, for his new cable television network. However, films by independents were still in production and M-G-M was still a force to reckon with in distribution.

Left: *Hoods Danny DeVito and Joe Piscopo take orders from their boss, Dan Hedaya (left) in* Wise Guys *(1986).*

Above: *Gregory Hines (left) and Billy Crystal as the street smart cops in* Running Scared *(1986).*

Left: *The crowded cockpit of the flying RV in* Spaceballs *(1987) with (left to right) John Candy, Lorraine Shields, Daphne Zuniga and Bill Pullman.*

Below center: *Timothy Dalton and Olivia D'Abo escape in a cello case in* The Living Daylights *(1987).*

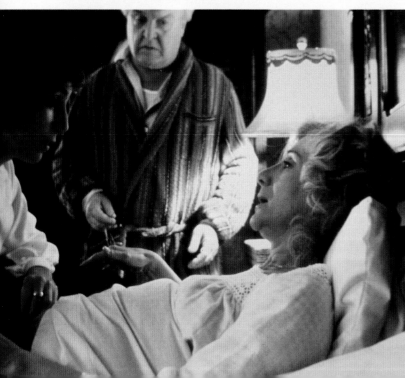

The first M-G-M release of 1987 was an extremely scary one. *Dead Of Winter* (1987) starred Mary Steenburgen as an aspiring actress who auditions in an isolated mansion for what she believes is a part. Actually she is to take the place of a dead kidnap victim. The film costarred Jan Rubes as the mysterious wheelchair-bound owner of the house in the country and Roddy McDowell as the requisite sinister man-servant. The screenplay by Marc Shmuger and Mark Malone and the direction by Arthur Penn managed to make a 'damsel in distress' plot seem fresh and frightening.

Spaceballs (1987) was Mel Brooks's send-up of *Star Wars*. The cast included Rick Moranis as Dark Helmet, a villain overpowered by his head gear; John Candy as Barf, half-man, half-dog and his own best friend; mime Lorraine Shields as Dot Matrix (voice by Joan Rivers); a female C3PO and maid to the Druish Princess Vespa (Daphne Zuniga); Bill Pullman as Lone Star, a 'space bum;' and Dom DeLuise as the voice of Pizza the Hutt. As usual in a Mel Brooks film, the plot didn't matter, the sight gags kept coming (the Millennium Falcon had been replaced with a flying RV), and Mel Brooks, playing both the wise and wizened Yoghurt and President Skroob of the planet Spaceball, had a better time than anyone else.

The next James Bond picture marked the advent of a new Bond, as Timothy Dalton took over the role of 007 in *The Living Daylights* (1987). Directed by John Glen, and based on a short story by Ian Fleming, the screenplay by Michael G Wilson concerned a defecting Russian general, a crooked American arms dealer, a beautiful cellist who doubles as an assassin, and the war in Afghanistan. The gimmicks provided by Q included a key that could open 90 percent of the locks in the world, and a gadget filled with a gas that stunned its victim when activated by the tune of 'Rule Britannia.' There seemed to be fewer women in Bond's life this time around, and Dalton was a much more serious and saturnine spy than his predecessors.

A surprise success for the studio was *Moonstruck* (1987), a light and charming comedy directed by Norman Jewison. The plot involved an Italian-American widow, played by Cher, who is engaged (sensibly she thinks) to 'Mr Johnny

Cammareri' (Danny Aiello) but subsequently falls in love with his brother (Nicolas Cage). Subplots concerned the extramarital affair of her father, played by Vincent Gardenia, and a potential fling not undertaken by her mother, played by Olympia Dukakis. The screenplay, written by John Patrick Shanley, won an Academy Award. Awards for Best Actress and Best Supporting Actress were won by Cher and Ms Dukakis respectively. These were the first Academy Awards won by an M-G-M production since Richard Dreyfuss won for *The Goodbye Girl* (1977).

Willow (1988), a fantasy conceived and produced by George Lucas and directed by Ron Howard, told the story of a young hero who saved the life and kingdom of a princess, overthrowing the evil usurper with the aid of some strange and unenthusiastic allies. The hero, well-played by Warwick Davis was a small person, and the princess at risk was even smaller – a baby in fact. One of the allies was a witch who spent most of the film as a muskrat. Two others were actually seen as elves. If the *Star Wars* saga had not been so successful, *Willow* might have been better received. But magic had become an expected ingredient in a Lucas film, and not even a good two-headed dragon, and the evil queen played by Jean Marsh, could remind the audience that a 'quest' was a universal concept and did not necessarily require space hardware and quick intercutting.

One of the most successful films produced by M-G-M in the eighties was the hilarious *A Fish Called Wanda* (1988). Written by and starring former Monty Python member John Cleese, the plot revolved around a band of jewel thieves – the incredibly thick Otto ('Don't call me stupid'), played by Kevin Kline; the delectable Wanda Gerschwitz, played by Jamie Lee Curtis; and the animal-loving, stuttering Ken, played by

Michael Palin. Crucial to the plot was Wanda's seduction of the very proper English barrister Archie Leach, played by Cleese, with whom she eventually falls in love. The film was brilliantly directed by Charles Crichton, a veteran of the Ealing comedies of the 1950s. Kevin Kline's riotous performance earned him the Academy Award for Best Supporting Actor.

The Mighty Quinn (1989), an unusual mystery based on the novel *Finding Maubee* by A Z H Carr, starred Denzel Washington in the title role as the police chief of a West Indian island who must hunt for an elusive childhood friend who may be being framed for murder. The film, directed by Carl Schenkel with a screenplay by Hampton Fancher, featured a strong cast including M Emmett Walsh, James Fox, and Robert Townsend as the mysterious Maubee, as well as a captivating reggae score and beautiful photography.

Above right: *Denzel Washington (left) as the policeman Quinn and Robert Townsend as the mysterious Maubee in* The Mighty Quinn *(1989).*

Right: *Wanda (Jamie Lee Curtis) and Archie (John Cleese) are watched from a balcony window by Otto (Kevin Kline) in* A Fish Called Wanda *(1988).*

Opposite bottom: *Loretta Castorini (Cher) gets advice from her parents, played by Vincent Gardenia and Olympia Dukakis, in* Moonstruck *(1987).*

A Dry White Season (1989), based on the novel by Ardie Brink, was a serious study of one white South African's realization of the cruelty of apartheid as he becomes involved with tracing the disappearance of his gardener's son. Donald Sutherland, in one of his few sympathetic roles, starred as the schoolteacher Ben du Toit, and the supporting cast included Janet Suzman as his wife and Winston Ntshona as the gardener. Marlon Brando made a cameo appearance (his first in a film since 1980) as an activist lawyer recruited by du Toit who is hoping to overturn the verdict of suicide placed on the gardener and his son, who both died of torture in police custody. Although the film is, perhaps, too simplistic, it was one of the first films to show the life of both whites and blacks in South Africa. The director was Euzhan Palcy, and the screenplay was by Palcy and Colin Welland, who also wrote *Chariots of Fire* (Allied Star/Enigma, 1981).

In 1990, Kirk Kerkorian finally managed to sell for $1.3 billion (less that the price paid by Ted Turner only five years before) what remained of the great studio he had purchased

Top left: *Janet Suzman and Donald Sutherland starred in* A Dry White Season *(1989).*
Opposite: *Robert de Niro gives Jane Fonda a ride on his bike in* Stanley and Iris *(1990).*

Left: *Michelle Pfeiffer and Sean Connery in Red Square in* The Russia House *(1990).*

in 1969. The buyer was Pathé Communications, a European conglomerate owned by Italian financier Giancarlo Parretti. The company was renamed MGM Pathé Communications, and Mr Parretti vowed to make the M-G-M lion 'roar again.'

Stanley and Iris (1990), one of the studio's few releases of that year, was a quiet love story about two blue collar workers in a bakery in Waterbury, Connecticut. Stanley is illiterate, and when Iris discovers the fact, which he has been trying to hide through various subterfuges, she teaches him to read. Jane Fonda and Robert DeNiro gave sympathetic performances in the starring roles, and were ably supported by Swoosie Kurtz, Martha Plimpton, and Feodor Chaliapin, who played DeNiro's aging father. The script was written by the husband and wife team of Harriet Frank and Irving Ravetch, and the film was ably directed by Martin Ritt.

John Le Carre's *The Russia House* (1990) starred Sean Connery as writer Barley Blair and Michelle Pfeiffer as Katya, the beautiful Russian who has been entrusted with a manuscript which analyzes the Russian defense system. This, of course, is of interest to all the intelligence services in the West. Although these grey men may be treated as stereotypes (the English are crafty, the Americans are crude), Le Carre as always created a believable, if sad, world, and the novel was cleverly brought to the screen by playwright Tom Stoppard and director Fred Schepisi.

In 1991, Mr Parretti was unable to meet the payments incurred in his purchase of M-G-M, and a court in Delaware awarded control of the studio to the French bank Credit Lyonnais. The bank, with a wisdom that hindsight seems to indicate was absent from previous management, allowed business to continue, feeling perhaps that the best way to get money out of a movie company was to allow it to make movies. Producers continued to work on films in production and films continued to be released.

Despite cash flow problems which delayed releases of a number of films, M-G-M struck it rich with one film released that summer. *Thelma And Louise* (1991), which starred Susan Sarandon as Louise and Geena Davis as Thelma, has variously been described as a feminist tract, a female buddy movie, and a female road movie. It may be all of these, but in the capable hands of director Ridley Scott, working from the screenplay by Callie Khouri, it became much more. The difficulties that the two women find piling up on them, beginning with the unpremeditated murder of the good ol' boy who is trying to rape Thelma, seem to be inevitable, the result of the way these women have been treated and expect to be treated by a collection of the most revolting men to ever hit the screen, all of whom are most believable in their swinish qualities. There are two sympathetic male characters, Louise's boyfriend Jimmy (Michael Madsen) and Hal (Harvey Keitel), the police officer who seems to understand how the whole sorry story happened. In the hands of a less talented director, the low budget film might well have sunk, but Ridley Scott gave it a polish and beauty that transcended what might have been sordid and turned it into that rare thing – a movie that both entertained and made the audience think.

The Cutting Edge (1992) was a film about the seemingly incompatible pairing of a former hockey player (D B Sweeney) and a spoiled figure skater (Moira Kelly) who end up in Olympic competition together. The timing of the release, which coincided with the 1992 Winter Olympics, brought favorable box office receipts, and the crisp cutting of the skating sequences was beautifully handled. The director was Paul M Glaser, and the screenplay was written by Tony Gilroy.

Of Mice And Men (1992) was a skillful remake in color of the classic 1940 film starring Lon Chaney and Burgess Meredith. The new adaptation of John Steinbeck's novella was written by Horton Foote and directed by Gary Sinise, who also played George. The role of his retarded friend, Lennie, was played by John Malkovich, who had costarred in the stage version of *The Grapes of Wrath* with Sinise in 1980. Sinise had been granted the film rights to *Of Mice And Men* by Mrs Steinbeck, because she was so impressed by the stage production. The story of two drifting laborers during the Depression had taken on new immediacy in light of the plight of the homeless in the 1990s, and the story was beautifully served by the production.

In 1991, Credit Lyonnais had appointed Alan Ladd, Jr, who had grown up in the business and had worked at a number of major studios, to head M-G-M. Ladd was managing to bring out movies that seemed to pay their way, and at one point in 1992 was even negotiating to take over Orion, one of the most successful of the new independents. To many people, the name M-G-M would always mean movies, and it didn't matter if they were not made on the old lot at Culver City. The old lion was clearly not finished yet.

Above: *Susan Sarandon and Geena Davis starred in* Thelma and Louise *(1991).*
Right: Of Mice and Men *(1992) starred Gary Sinise (left) and John Malkovich as George and Lennie.*

Opposite: *D B Sweeney and Moira Kelly skate together at the Olympics in the finale of* The Cutting Edge *(1992).*

INDEX

Numbers in italics refer to illustrations.